ABOUT THE AUTHOR

Shah Rukh Nadeem is an Expert Generalist who has been part of the corporate industry since 13 years now. His forte is product management, operations, channel development, growth and startups. He is currently leading a cutting-edge digital HR company, MyHCM Pakistan, as a Chief Executive Officer. He also teaches at several leading business schools in Karachi as a visiting faculty, especially courses pertaining to Entrepreneurship and Marketing. Shah Rukh has several aspects to his personality where he is also a master trainer and a corporate management consultant. Apart from all this, his social media presence as "Book Buddy" is what gained him fame amongst the youth of Pakistan. He is regarded as the premier Booktuber in the country. Shah Rukh has the most loyal family of followers (200,000+) across different social media platforms who regularly follow his video book reviews and posts. He is an individual who is passionate about the idea of making people read, learn, progress and self-actualize.

Shah Rukh can be approached through the following mediums

Website: www.bookbuddy.com.pk
Facebook: @bookbuddy
Instagram: @bookbuddyofficial
YouTube: Book Buddy
Email: shahrukh@bookbuddy.com.pk

READISTAN

Fifty of the best books compressed in One

SHAH RUKH NADEEM

Published by Liberty Publishing

C-16, Sector 31-A, Mehran Town Extension, Korangi Industrial Area, Karachi, Pakistan

www.libertybooks.com

First published in Pakistan 2022

Copyright © 2022 Shah Rukh Nadeem

The views and opinions expressed in this book are the author's own and the facts are as reported by him, and the publishers are not in any way liable for the same. The opinions expressed in our published works are those of the author(s) and do not reflect the opinions of Liberty Publishing.

ISBN 978-627-7626-037

TABLE OF CONTENTS

TABLE OF CONTENTS

TABLE OF CONTENTS

TABLE OF CONTENTS

TABLE OF CONTENTS

PREFACE

"A man is but the product of his thoughts. What he thinks he becomes." Let me take this statement a step further and say that a man is a product of his thoughts and circumstances. Let me further establish what I wrote and culminate this into one single statement which defines the philosophy of my life: "A man is but the product of his thoughts and circumstances, which he has the power to mould in any way he wants. Therefore, whatever happens in our life is a result of our thoughts, actions and decisions." I am a strong believer in the fact that humans have an inherent volcanic potential which enables them to carve out their future and define their destiny themselves. Since childhood, I have heard people talking about luck (Kismet) and a demarcated destiny that we humans are slaves of. Even at the tender age of 8, I wasn't able to absorb and acknowledge the strange and indispensable case of destiny which people thought holds our lives together. Determinism as a philosophical thought never attracted me and I always wondered how on earth we can be so helpless and surrender our lives to our destiny; despite possessing such mercurial physical, emotional, intellectual and cognitive skills. Through experience came learning, through learning came wisdom and through wisdom came the realisation of the potential that a person carries within them. This made me come to a very solid conclusion in life that it is not in the stars to hold our destiny, but in ourselves.

I have always had a very strong internal locus of control which has helped me in navigating through life. This might sound pompous or narcissistic to some of you but the aim of interacting with you through this book is not to mince my words and take you to a fairy land. Rather, I want to apprise you about the core learnings of my life, with the hope that you can either relate to them or learn from them.

A few of you who know me through my social media presence are well aware of my mission in life pertaining to reading and lifelong learning. For the people who are getting to know me through this book for the first time, I welcome you from the core of my heart. What you will read in the next couple of hundred pages is a part of me. It's the literature that has shaped me as a thoughtful individual and has significantly expanded my horizon and wavelength of thinking. I owe a lot of my cognitive, emotional and intellectual development to the books that I have shared with all of you in this compilation.

Books and I go a long way back to the time when as a young boy I used to read Roald Dahl, Jules Verne and Charles Dickens. I still remember two novels that fascinated me to the core in childhood: "Danny the Champion of the World" by Roald Dahl and "20,000 Leagues Under The Sea" by Jules Verne. This was the start of my love affair with book reading which has spanned over more than two decades now. People often ask me how I find time for reading. My answer is very simple; reading over the years has become a part of me similar to the way we eat, sleep, walk and talk. It doesn't take much effort to open a book and start reading. However, this is not something that has happened miraculously overnight. It has taken years of strict regimen, sacrifice and sheer hard work to reach this stage in life. From my experience, I have concluded that falling in love with boredom is one of the key ingredients for developing a reading habit and maintaining focus in life, which subsequently leads to success.

The modern century breeds instant gratification. People these days have an attention span shorter than a goldfish. Therefore, they tend to seek immediate results without putting in gruelling man-hours of hard work. In order to develop the habit of reading, you need to fall in love with the concept of boredom, where you are turning pages after pages; day in day out. The wisdom embedded in the books you read will eventually transform you and your personality in ways that you can't even imagine. I have a first-hand experience of what reading does to your heart, mind, soul and intellect. It nourishes you, completes you and makes you an unstoppable force. It helps you realise and identify the potential hidden inside your genetic code, so you can unleash yourself and do justice to the capabilities you possess.

"Why did I name this book Readistan?" There is a solid logic behind it. Book Buddy is one of the greatest passions of my life which is driven by the obsession to stimulate the intellectual muscles of my followers. It is an effort to inculcate and promote a sense of rationality, progressive mindset, learning ability and the quest to achieve self-actualization through reading and learning. I am a strong advocate of the fact that life holds limitless potential and possibilities for anyone willing to go the extra mile. I want to be that agent of change for people who want to develop themselves into exemplary individuals through a lifetime of reading and learning. This journey started in the year 2018, and the goal is to continue it till my last breath. Readistan is an endeavour from my side to instill the habit of reading in our people, so they can have a fulfilling and well-informed life.

The following is my vision regarding my platform Book Buddy and this book Readistan:

- Bring the best literature which has been written across the globe to people so that it opens new perspectives of thinking.
- Let the people know about the stalwarts of history who have made it big through their positive personality attributes. It will help people learn and imbibe some of their character and personality traits.
- Promote reading and learning culture in the country.
- Promote pluralism and rationality of thought in our nation.
- Help people in attaining a state of self-actualization through identification of their hidden potential and making the best use of it.
- Develop tolerance and patience in people to have progressive discourse and respect for each other's opinions.

As I said earlier, our thoughts shape who we are. But if we take a step back and question ourselves, what shapes our thoughts? While there can be many philosophical answers to this question, but to be objective, a lot of our thoughts are shaped by the sort of active and vicarious learning we do in our daily life. If you ask me, one of the biggest catalysts behind the development of mature thinking is to learn from the literature that has been written around the world. This book is an effort to bring my readers the wonders of reading by consolidating the wisdom of 50 books that have helped shape my life in a better way. The book is a blend of various genres of literature including Philosophy, Psychology, Politics, History, Biography, Autobiography, Self-help and Business Management.

It has taken a gargantuan effort to read all these books, synthesise their core ideas and then present them in my own words to you. Through "Readistan" I have made it possible for you to read a single book in just a matter of 10 minutes. This is my effort to make my people read, learn, progress and self-actualize.

I hope you find the book useful and meaningful. Somewhere, if the words I have written can help you improve and transform your life, I will feel my purpose has been served. Best wishes to all of you.

Happy Reading!

THE STORY OF MY LIFE

The next few pages come from the core of my heart. They may also give you the ultimate motivation that you might need in life.

It's 46° C in the sweltering heat of Bahawalpur; a beautiful, modern and historical city in Southern Punjab. Due to its proximity to the nearby Cholistan desert, the summers in the city are harsh and oppressive. My younger brother Taimur has just returned from the Tandoor. Due to his resilience and patience, he was always given the task of going to the Tandoor with home-kneaded flour to get the *rotis* baked. Most of the Pakistanis are well aware of what a Tandoor is but for anyone who doesn't know, it is a sort of oven that is commercially used to make a *roti*. In Punjab, there is a practice where households send their own "Ata" (flour), to get the *rotis* baked. Back in the late 90's, it used to cost only 1 rupee to get two *rotis* made but getting that one rupee was sadly a struggle.

****

This was an existential shock of sorts, since never in our lives while living in Karachi did we face any financial obstructions. Life was so blissful and privileged when we were children. My father was living a life tantamount to the American Dream in Karachi. He hailed from a small town named Bahawalnagar and in his hustle days migrated to Karachi, back in the year 1978, to carve out his future. He had worked hard to earn a respectable living and was indeed a source of envy back in his hometown, where people used to say *"Farrakkh* (his name was Farrukh and in Punjabi, everyone used to refer to him as Farrakkh) *nu wekho, bari changi life guzaar reya ae. Sariyaan bacheyaan nu angrezi school ich daakhil karaya ae"* which loosely translates to "Just look at Farrukh- he is living such a good life. He has admitted all his kids in an English medium school." Getting enrolled in an English Medium school back in the day was a big deal and that too, not one or two, but five children. All five of us used to study in The City School which even today is one of the most prestigious and expensive institutions in the country.

My father invested all his earnings in us without thinking about what the future will entail. Giving us the best lifestyle, schooling, perks and privileges of life is what his life revolved around. When people were busy buying real estate, he, on the other hand, was busy developing us as mature and thinking individuals. I do not remember him ever buying anything for himself.

Without being pompous, I can say that the way my father brought me up was exceptional, a style that can easily be benchmarked. He was not only a friend but also a companion. During my childhood, he was a serious task master. I remember the innumerable thrashings I got from him, but as I continued to grow, he transitioned into the friendliest human being ever. He made sure to give me all the support he never got.

It's a funny analogy but I really want to give it since it's very relatable. Many of you must have seen the iconic movie "Dilwale Dulhaniya Le Jayengay." In the movie, Anupam Kher plays Shahrukh Khan's father who supports him through thick and thin. He says to him that *Jo main nahi kar paya woh mera beta karega.*" (What I couldn't do, my son will do it). Whenever I hear this dialogue, it feels as if my father is saying it to me. The funny part is that he was not very expressive in terms of voicing fatherly love but his actions showed how much love and care he had for all of us.

He was at the peak of his career in the year 1995. This was the time when Karachi was going through the worst period of its history. The political turmoil and riots created so much pressure that my father contemplated migrating back to Punjab, and eventually, we did. This was at that time the worst decision we made as a family which led to the most challenging time of our lives. From living a luxurious life in Karachi to not even a place we could call home. When we shifted to Bahawalpur my father started a medicine business. Everything worked smoothly for a year but the business eventually died down. During that time we were living a nomadic life, shifting from Bahawalpur to Lal-Suhanra to Rahim Yar Khan and then back to Bahawalpur again. Gradually, we lost all our assets and the only thing left was a 1990 model Suzuki FX car.

My father once again took a leap of faith by selling his car and invested that money in establishing a restaurant in Rahim Yar Khan with his partner Sadiq whom we lovingly call Sadiq Uncle. The restaurant got off to a flying start and it seemed as if the tough time was behind us. However, our good days were numbered. After a year of successful running, it too lost the hype and in a matter of months hit rock bottom. My father consulted his partner and decided to make his way back to Karachi (the land of opportunity) and start his life from square one.

After enrolling in one of the best schools in the country, there came a time when my father couldn't afford to pay the fee of even a single child, let alone for all five of us. As a result, all of us had to take a gap year. Though we weren't able to afford the school fee, our parents made sure that we continue to get our weekly "Sunday Dawn Newspaper" so that our English learning and General Knowledge is not compromised. Today when people ask me the secret to my command in English language, I attribute it all to my parents especially in this case my mother. She had an infatuation with the thought of her children being well-spoken in English.

Eventually, my father made it back to Karachi while we stayed back in Bahawalpur. Back in Karachi, he had to restart his life at the age of 45. When I imagine it today, I get tears in my eyes visualizing my 45-year-old father changing two buses on his way to reach office.

Whereas, my mother used to get Rs. 100 every day in Bahawalpur to run the show. Kudos to her mercurial managerial skills, my mother did a great job in those mere 100 rupees. I still remember that the only thing we could afford in breakfast was a paratha and green yoghurt. This was the same time when it was hard to gather even 5 rupees to get the *rotis* made from the Tandoor. That time is etched in my heart and soul. Though we could hardly make both ends meet, yet my parents never made us realise that something was wrong. They nurtured our mindset in a way that we always felt liberated, happy, future-oriented and progressive. When I grew up, I realised that these are the character traits of a winner. I have observed in life that the majority of the people who face tough circumstances either fall into deep alleys of regret or are disturbed psychologically for life. On the other hand, my parents even in the toughest of circumstances continued to nurture us as strong individuals. The learnings of those times have shaped me into who I am today.

As time passed by, we siblings disseminated into various cities to keep ourselves afloat and somehow continue our studies. I went to Lahore, then Bahawalnagar; my sister also went to Bahawalnagar where we were joined by my brother Taimur as well. Here I want to specially thank my uncle, my father's younger brother Anju Chachu, who was kind enough to support us in our studies at that time. You know what, when I look back, I not only thank the people who supported me and my father but also have gratitude for the people who were indifferent to our suffering because in some way or the other, they helped me grow as an individual. During those times of turmoil, my father continued to support me in every way and made me the individual I am today. I have seen the harshest and also the best of times with him. He made me bold, confident and assertive.

He also had the most incredible set of friends I have ever seen. I have never seen a group of friends who are so sincerely connected to each other. When the chips were down at my father's end, no family member came forward in the way his friends did. They were with him each step of the way, partners in good times and ultimate supporters in arduous circumstances. Two individuals are worth mentioning here, Aftab Uncle and Danish Uncle who were his confidants and ultimate support system. Danish Uncle is one of the angels in our life. I have never seen such a generous, kind and selfless gentleman. He was with my father till my father breathed his last. I don't have words to express the colossal contribution that Uncle has had in our lives.

With the passage of time, our family started recovering financially. When my father came back to Karachi, he had no vehicle to commute and was dependent on public transport. After a few months, he could only afford to buy a Vespa Scooter. I remember amusingly doing wheelies on that Scooter. As years went by, he bought a car, then another and then another. There was a time when we simultaneously had four cars in the house. He got my sisters married, sent one of my brothers to Saudi Arabia for business and the youngest one to England for higher studies. He started to travel abroad with my mother for vacations. Life was back on track, due to his persistence in the toughest of circumstances.

When I was going through these hard-hitting times, it really was strenuous but in hindsight, I think it was a blessing in disguise. It helped me understand very early in life the meaning of hard work, struggle, persistence and the art of facing adversity. Today, If I can talk in front of hundreds of people, make YouTube videos, teach, lead a company or write a book it's because of all those difficulties that shaped my character very early in life. My parents gave me the initial head start in life that they perhaps couldn't get and then I was on my own, flying high in the sky.

It was my parents' ultimate desire to see me as an engineer and like most of the people in our country I imbibed their dream in myself. After finishing my Intermediate, I got admission in Sir Syed University in Karachi in the Electronics Engineering department. Very soon after admission, I realised that it was not my cup of tea from any stretch of imagination. I tried to put my heart and soul in my studies, but engineering was just not me. I am a man of social sciences, I love interaction with people, I love human psychology and there is no room for circuitry and transistors in my life. I dragged my presence in the University for one year before calling it a day.

The realisation came to me that I will be wasting my time, effort and money in pursuit of a degree which will hold no value for me. The only good memory I have of Sir Syed University is the first prize I got in the English Declamation contest which made me an overnight star on campus.

My decision to quit engineering came as an absolute shock to my parents who were devastated, especially my mother. However, I gathered myself very soon and enrolled myself for a business degree. In hindsight, I can very confidently say that it was the best decision of my life. That single decision contributed towards my overall personality and social upliftment. Since that time onwards, I haven't looked back.

There is a reason why I have told you this story of mine. My personal story gave me the motivation to take life seriously and make it count. I have seen the best and the worst. Today, I can sip a cup of tea sitting in a shabby old roadside café and be at peace, and can also lead a conference and enjoy dinner with distinguished dignitaries in Michelin star hotels of the world. This maturity of thought and character has come through due to my experiences and my upbringing. I don't want to call my story a rags to riches one, since the term is quite clichéd now. Rather, in my humble opinion, it has been an exhilarating journey of learning and gaining experience. If my story can inspire any one of you, I will feel my purpose is served.

Let's get started!

HOW THE BOOK IS ORGANISED

The book reviews are presented in a succinct yet comprehensive manner. The language used is deliberately chosen to be easy so that even the most difficult of concepts are easy to understand.

 Each book review starts with its main learning or essence mentioned on the left-hand side of the page. This gives you a brief overview of what the book is all about.

 Each book review starts by mentioning the name of the book, its author and the genre it belongs to.

 Most important text or key takeaway which requires meticulous attention has been mentioned in a separate column so that readers can take note of it.

 Use this space to write your notes and key takeaways from the book.

HE WHO HAS A WHY TO LIVE FOR, CAN DEAL WITH ANY HOW

MAN'S SEARCH FOR MEANING
Author : Dr. Victor E. Frankl
Genre: Philosophy

One philosophical conjecture that continues to enthrall people of all ages comes in the form of a question, "What is the purpose of our life?" "Why are we born?" Is our existence in this world meaningless and purposeless or is there a deep, profound meaning ingrained in life? For centuries philosophers and scientists have been striving hard to find the answer to this question pertaining to existential crisis. A few people have been rather successful in answering this conjecture as well. However, amongst all these remarkable stalwarts, there is a psychologist and a philosopher who, with the help of his magnum opus book "Man's Search For Meaning", has described the purpose of life with so much clarity, depth, and truthfulness that nobody has ever done before. His name is Dr. Viktor Frankl.

This book has sold more than 10 million copies due to its awe-inspiring content which has spanned generations. Before I discuss the main elements of the book, let's put things into perspective and shed some light on the life history of Dr. Frankl. He was an Austrian psychiatrist, philosopher and holocaust survivor who, along with his family, was put into brutal and violent concentration camps by Nazi forces. During his confinement, Dr. Frankl's mother, father, wife and brother were cruelly tortured and eventually murdered. Even after these direful and dreadful events, Dr. Frankl not only lived a fulfilling life but also wrote an immortal book in the form of Man's Search For Meaning. It's not merely a book but a philosophy, a formula for life with which you can achieve the depth of your existence; eventually leading you towards the identification of the real purpose of your life.

Dr. Frankl was inspired by German philosopher, Fredrick Nietzsche's following quote:

> He who has a why to live for,
> can deal with any how!

This quote suggests that an individual who has found his purpose of existence and identity can deal undauntingly with any hardship that life has to offer. This is the reason why even after facing such pain, cruelty, atrocity and injustice in life, he never lost hope and led a successful life. His time in prison gave him the most profound understanding of human psychology. During his confinement, he observed that those prisoners who were pessimistic and didn't have any hope of a brighter and better future gradually started getting ill and eventually succumbed to the hardships and brutalities of the camp.

Another reality dawned on him during his time at the Nazi concentration camp. He came to realise that a person gets to know about the purpose of his life during his worst circumstances when the chips are down and he has hit rock bottom. The ones who give up during these strenuous circumstances lose their race of life while those who remain steadfast, committed, courageous and dedicated eventually become successful. He writes that our life has certain expectations from us and the individual who understands these expectations prospers.

One of the most significant contributions of Dr. Frankl in the field of psychology is the introduction of Logotherapy, a concept he talks about in detail in this book. With the help of logotherapy, he helped many of his patients by fulfilling their search for finding purpose in life. According to logotherapy, the best quality a human being possesses is his "free will" which means independent thinking. Every individual has full authority and freedom to live his

According to logotherapy, the best quality a human being possesses is his "free will" which means independent thinking. Every individual has full authority and freedom to live his life on his own terms.

life on his own terms. Logotherapy works wonders for people in terms of improving their overall mental health. It helps them identify the skills required to identify the gap that exists between their present and their future, and then work relentlessly towards narrowing that gap as much as possible. Therefore, a fulfilling life is actually a continuous struggle to achieve a worthy ideal. One should keep striving hard to become the best version of himself. Dr. Frankl's logotherapy enables a person to achieve self-actualization; a concept popularized by famous psychologist Abraham Maslow in his famous research paper published in 1943 with the title "A Theory of Human Motivation."

Another remarkable concept propagated by the great author in the book is that every person wants to be happy in life and a large majority of us spend our lives in pursuit of happiness. However, he believes that this is not the right way to approach life. He states that the actual source of happiness is to delve into some work or hobby which enables you to even forget yourself. This is the reason why scientists, painters, sculptors and artists remain content in life since their interest becomes their profession vis-a-vis the people who work monotonously day in day out just to pay their bills. Therefore, one of the key determinants which can give meaning to your life is to pursue a passion, a hobby or anything of your interest which can give direction to your life and keep you happy and contented.

Here a million-dollar question arises: How can you search for the purpose of life? This isn't a very easy question to answer. However, Dr. Frankl expresses a very interesting way to seek the answer to this question. As a psychologist, whenever he used to be visited by patients for consultancy, he used to ask them a very unusual question point-blank, "Why do you not commit suicide?" He writes that many patients had a very solid answer to this outrageous and unfamiliar

question. Taking this as a starting and pivotal point, he used to transform their meaningless and purposeless life into a meaningful one. Through his therapy, he untangled many minds and gave them a reason to live.

This was all about "Man's Search for Meaning" and its main concepts. According to my observation, majority of the people I meet on an everyday basis are truly clueless about the purpose of their existence. Some perennially keep seeking the answer to the question, "Is there a purpose attached to our life or not?" It's painful to see that innumerable people are living a directionless life without having an idea that they have a debt to pay back to life.

There surely is a purpose attached to our existence in this world. However, if you have failed to find that purpose as you read these lines don't worry at all. This is referred to as existential frustration. It is a feeling of being restless, uneasy or unsatisfied. The good news for all of you is that it's not a negative feeling at all. You have to nurture and protect this feeling. This feeling in itself will be your beacon and will lead you towards glory. Remember, action cures fear. Be curious, dynamic and keep going in life through pragmatic actions. Existential crisis occurs when our society, our environment, our family, our friends and our colleagues tell us how to live our life. When you start living your life according to the wavelength prescribed by society, chances are you will be unhappy. Therefore, if you really want to achieve happiness and fulfill the ultimate purpose of your life then do things that you are passionate about. The goal of life should not be to get a luxury car, a big house, a world tour or uncountable wealth; rather life becomes beautiful and worth living when it has challenges and your fixation and madness to trump those challenges. If you keep on following Dr. Frankl's theory of life, I guarantee you will soon be on your way to living a purpose-driven and meaningful life.

Existential crisis occurs when our society, our environment, our family, our friends and our colleagues tell us how to live our life. When you start living your life according to the wavelength prescribed by society, chances are you will be unhappy.

PERSONAL NOTES

Use this space to write your notes and key takeaways from the book.

FAIL, FAIL FAST, FAIL FORWARD

STARTUP NATION
Author: Dan Senor & Saul Singer
Genre: Business Management

Since childhood, I have been hearing the statement *"Yahoodi Ki Sazish"* which translates to "conspiracy by the Jews." This is a clichéd disclosure that every Pakistani is well acquainted with. There was a time when the former Prime Minister of Pakistan Mr. Imran Khan was labeled as a covert agent of the Jews. Similarly, Valentine's Day in our country is also marked as a conspiracy by the Jews so that they can contaminate our culture. A few programmes in mass media, infact the entire media industry, are sometimes categorised as some sort of conspiracy by the Jews. Seemingly, Jews are responsible for every wrong and dubious thing happening in our country. While growing up, due to an immature thought process, I also used to believe that the people of Israel have nothing better to do except to conspire against a country like ours.

However, a few years back I took a pledge that I will never blindly believe in anything without profound research, observation, analysis and comprehensive understanding of the matter. Instead of believing in stereotypes and urban myths, I will find the truth by myself. This pledge completely transformed my wavelength of thinking and I began my research on Israel which is predominantly a country of Jews. After consolidating information, I was surprised to know that a small country with a population of only 9.2 Million (Year-2020) can be so powerful and influential.

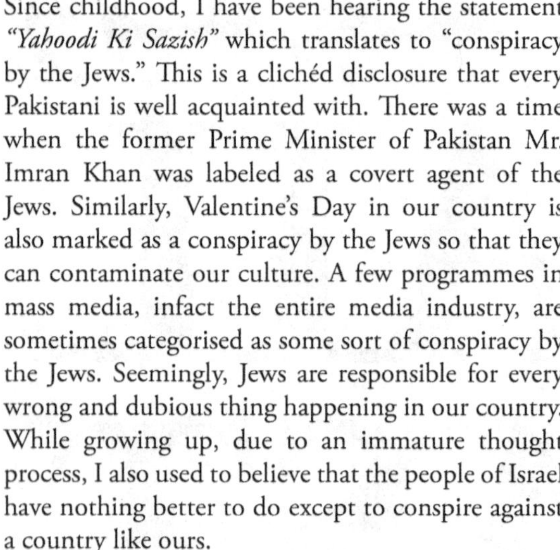

These facts made me more inquisitive to investigate the reason for the popularity of Jews and what makes them such a sought-after community. I was in the middle of my research when I found this book called Startup Nation which had answers to all of my questions. So, keeping aside bias, hatred, religious conflicts, jingoism and rhetoric let me summarise the reason behind the success of Israel and Jews. This comes with a disclaimer that I am not part of any Jewish conspiracy.

Israel is also known as a startup nation. A startup is a type of business that introduces a new idea or new to the world products in the market. The admirable thing about Israel is that it has the greatest number of startups per capita in the world. If we do some number crunching, it reveals that for every 1400 people there is one startup company. This means that this country has over 6000+ startups. This magnitude of entrepreneurial attitude is not present in any other country of the world.

The admirable thing about Israel is that it has the greatest number of startups per capita in the world. If we do some number crunching, it reveals that for every 1400 people there is one startup company. This means that this country has over 6000+ startups.

Another testament to this fact is that after USA, the greatest number of listed companies on NASDAQ (2nd biggest stock exchange globally) are from Israel. These are not small companies, rather companies worth billions of dollars. These statistics were good enough to get me hooked and have a deeper dive to find out the reason behind their success. In the following paragraphs, I have elaborated on five main reasons from this book "Startup Nation" that have made these people so accomplished, economically and socially.

1. One of the biggest reasons for the success of Israel is that its people live their lives according to a principle which goes like this: "Fail, Fail Fast, Fail Forward." In Israeli society people are appreciated for their failures, risk-taking is encouraged and initiative is fully supported. If you look at other countries of the world, especially those belonging to the third world, failure in business or other venture of life is tantamount to a proverbial death sentence which is backed by maligning and slander. The quality

One of the biggest reasons for the success of Israel is that its people live their lives according to a principle which goes like this: "Fail, Fail Fast, Fail Forward." In Israeli society people are appreciated for their failures, risk-taking is encouraged and initiative is fully supported.

of the Jewish nation is that they are not afraid of initiatives and are very comfortable in taking risks because they are aware that even if they fail, their society will give them multiple chances to succeed. This progressive element of their society makes the people of Israel fearless which eventually helps them become successful in business.

2. Strong focus on research and development is another reason behind their success. There is no match for Jews when it comes to excellence in research. The following two things attest to this fact.

Strong focus on research and development is another reason behind their success. There is no match for Jews when it comes to excellence in research.

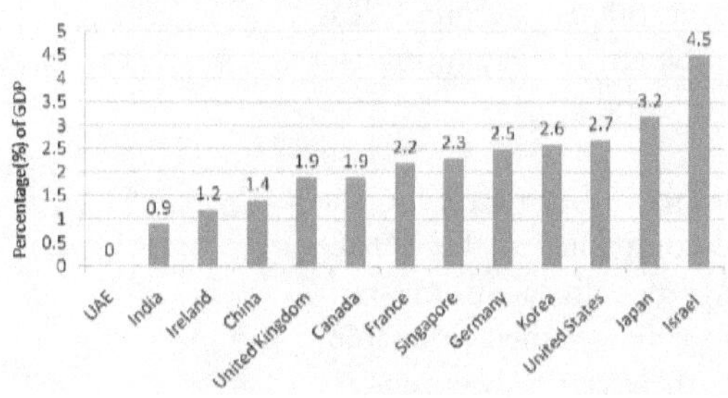

Source: United Nations Development Programme Report 2007/2008.

The above graph is an illustration of the expenditure on research and development as a percentage of GDP by the different leading countries of the world. It clearly depicts that Israel leads the score card here. The second testament of their strong focus on R&D is that research centers of leading technology companies of the world like Google, Amazon, Microsoft and Facebook are present in Israel. Whenever these tech giants have to make a new product, they conceive and research the idea in Israel and then ship it across the world. This happens because Jews are instinctively research-oriented, an attribute of their personality which these technology companies make full use of.

3. Israelis have a laser focus on education which is

another reason behind their success and prosperity. They specially focus on knowledge, brainpower and development of intellect so that they can find practical solutions to their societal problems. To strengthen their education infrastructure, they established science and technology institutes when the world was reeling with war and massacre. Technion Institute of Technology (EST.1912), Hebrew Science University (EST.1925) and Weizmann Institute of Science (EST.1934) speak volumes about their focus on scientific studies. This thought process has proved to be a game-changer for their nation. Following is a very classical example of what I have just stated. Israel always used to import war equipment, arms and ammunition. However, due to embargo they made a decision that it was better to start manufacturing all of it within the country. Therefore, they started manufacturing fighter jets known as Lavi. This project turned out to be too costly and hence had to be shelved in the year 1987. Due to the closure of this project, around 5000 scientists and engineers in the country became unemployed. Israeli society transformed this adversity into an opportunity. These 5000 scientists, instead of being dejected, entered the market, started working on technology and established new companies and startups. Hence, not only securing their future but contributing towards the growth of their country as well.

4. Chutzpah is a word in the English language derived from Hebrew which means boldness, assertiveness, confidence and a bit of arrogance. Chutzpah is another reason behind Israel's success. Their people do not believe in the status quo and can even take on their bosses if they go amiss. They never subdue their emotions by falling under pressure or being under the obligation of anyone. That is the reason why they sort out their societal issues quickly because their thinking is straight and to the point. Instead of merely giving lip service, they believe in practical and

pragmatic actions to take their lives forward.

5. Another reason for the success of this nation is mandatory military service. Every citizen of Israel is supposed to serve the military for two to three years. This helps them develop traits of leadership and self-reliance. Military service empowers them to make high-quality and quick decisions. These traits also assist them in developing successful businesses.

For my entire life, the only thing that reverberated around me was a feeling of negativity and hatred when it came to Israel. I am not at all advocating the fact that their success in business justifies their other abominable acts against humanity. However, I am a strong believer in the fact that when it comes to surviving and excelling in the modern world, we should keep our religious differences aside and learn even from our enemies. Wisdom demands an objective understanding of the issues based on facts and figures instead of focusing on non-objective and opinionated ranting of a few who influence the thinking of the masses by guiding them in the wrong way. I have always believed in objectivity and logic instead of emotional jingoism which is sans any intelligence. I am not in any way, advising you to replace your feeling of hatred towards Israel with feelings of acceptance or joy; that's not my job. My work is to enlighten you about the reasons which make a nation grow and achieve prosperity for its people. From here on in, you people are the best decision makers who have complete liberty to form your own opinions about what is right and what is wrong.

Wisdom demands an objective understanding of the issues based on facts and figures instead of focusing on non-objective and opinionated ranting of a few who influence the thinking of the masses by guiding them in the wrong way.

PERSONAL NOTES

Use this space to write your notes and key takeaways from the book.

PERSONAL NOTES

Use this space to write your notes and key takeaways from the book.

FIRST YOU MAKE HABITS AND THEN YOUR HABITS MAKE YOU

ATOMIC HABITS
Author: James Clear
Genre: Self-help

How successful you will be in your life depends a lot on the quality of your habits. It is rightly said that first you make habits and then your habits make you. Your trivial positive actions, if performed regularly, elevate you towards success while negative habits can plunge you towards failure. A lot of literature has been written on the importance of habits in our lives. However, the book that is considered a gold standard in this domain is a masterpiece by James Clear titled "Atomic Habits."

This book entails some of the most powerful concepts when it comes to our habits and is such a riveting read that it sweeps you off your feet. Try to read the next few paragraphs as meticulously as possible because they have the power to transform your life.

Atomic Habits is an international best seller and a very famous book in the self-help genre. The reason behind its super-hit status is its simple yet powerful concept. The author has communicated that by bringing atomic (small) improvements in our lives we can derive massive results. This can be illustrated with the following example:

The author has communicated that by bringing atomic (small) improvements in our lives we can derive massive results.

From 1908 till 2007, British cycling was going through its worst times and had hit rock bottom. In 95 years, it had only won one gold medal in the Olympics. Similarly, no British cyclist had ever won Tour de France which is considered to be the most prestigious cycling event. The reputation of the British cycling team was so tainted that top European bike manufacturers snubbed selling their equipment to British cyclists as it might hurt their

brand image. In this situation of turmoil came Sir Dave Brailsford as new performance director and turned the fate of the entire British cycling unit. Within just 5 years of his arrival, the British cycling team started dominating the cycling world.

In the 2008 Beijing Olympics cycling category, 60% of gold medals were won by the British team. In 2012 they further raised the bar by setting 9 Olympic records and 7 world records. In the same year Bradley Wiggins became the first British cyclist to win Tour de France. The next year, his teammate Chris Froome again won the title and repeated the feat till 2017. What actually did Dave Brailsford do to transform these ordinary cyclists into world-class athletes that broke all records? The answer is 1% improvement; meaning atomic improvement. Dave started improving minor things associated with cycling. For instance, he redesigned bike seats, improved the gear that cyclists used to wear, strengthened the grip of the tyres using alcohol, for quick muscle recovery he used massage gels and the list is never-ending. He did 1% improvement in all aspects of bicycling and all these atomic enhancements combined together to create massive improvements.

There is a general belief that massive success requires massive and abrupt change. However, in reality, we don't need earth-shattering change to accomplish success, rather we just need to improve 1% on a daily basis and the job is done.

There is a general belief that massive success requires massive and abrupt change. However, in reality, we don't need earth-shattering change to accomplish success, rather we only need to improve 1% on a daily basis and the job is done. This is exemplified in the following graph.

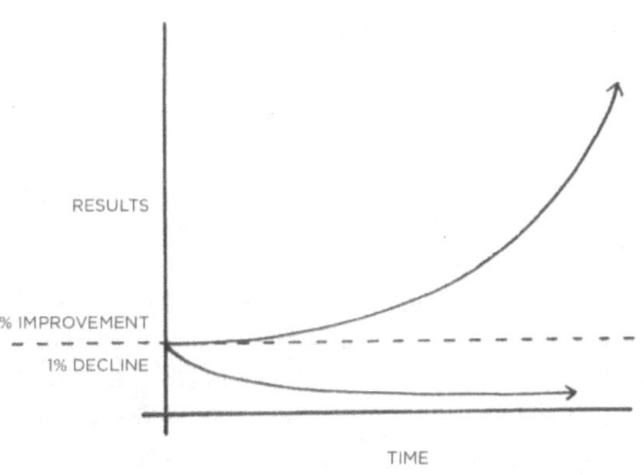

You can see time on X-Axis and results on Y-Axis. If you improve by just 1% every day then with the passage of time it compounds to exceptional growth and success leading you to become 37 times better than you are today in just a matter of a year. In case of just 1% deviation from the path, you will start losing your ground as time ticks along.

One of the pertinent things to question here is, "Why can't people hold their good habits for a long period of time?" For instance, they regularly go to the gym for a week and then falter behind or adopt a strict diet for a few days and then back to square one. This happens because of the Plateau of Latent Potential as visualised below.

THE PLATEAU OF LATENT POTENTIAL

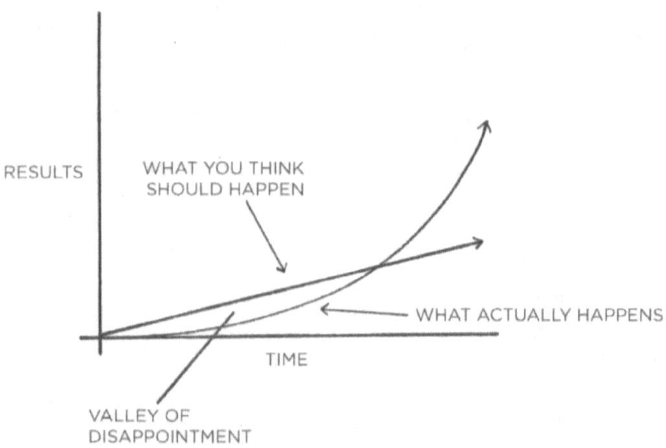

When we have to adopt a new habit, we expect the journey to be very straightforward and yield immediate results as a straight line. However, the reality is quite different. In order to see the best results of our habits we need perseverance and patience capital. A large majority puts in the work for a few days and then falls in the valley of disappointment, never enjoying the results of their

hard work. Remember, "habits are the compound interest of self-improvement." As you continue to practice high-quality habits over a long period of time you start witnessing high-quality results. It doesn't matter how successful or unsuccessful you are right now, what matters is whether your habits are putting you on the path towards success. If your trajectory is right and you are committed then, mark my words, you will be triumphant.

Remember, "habits are the compound interest of self-improvement." As you continue to practice high-quality habits over a long period of time you start witnessing high-quality results.

Another path-breaking concept that James Clear states in this book is regarding goals. In common knowledge, we always tend to say that a person should be visionary, ambitious and carry life goals. However, James Clear absolutely repudiates this claim. He insists that instead of focusing on goals, one should fall in love with the system of developing habits. On a goal-driven approach, he points out the following loopholes.

He insists that instead of focusing on goals, one should fall in love with the system of developing habits.

Problem # 1:

Winners and losers have the same goals. In every race, there will always be a winner and a loser. All the participants in a competition share the same goal and that is to win the race. Therefore, there is actually no difference between winning and losing. Instead of focusing on winning, focus on mastering the mechanics of the race and your journey will become effortless.

Problem # 2:

Achieving a goal is only a momentary change. You won the race; you achieved your goal and that's the end of the story. Therefore, goal is intrinsically fleeting.

Problem # 3:

Goals restrict your happiness. Until your goal is achieved you hold your happiness. You don't enjoy the process and the journey until the target is achieved. In case the goals are missed, the entire

Goals restrict your happiness. Until your goal is achieved you hold your happiness.

effort goes in vain and you continue to be regretful.

Problem # 4:
Goals are at odds with long-term progress. If you are a goal-oriented person then there is a high probability that as soon as you achieve your desired results you will stop your self-improvement and stop being progressive.

Another major concept articulated in this book is about behaviour change. According to the author, there are three layers of behaviour. One is outcome, second is processes and third is identity.

THREE LAYERS OF BEHAVIOR CHANGE

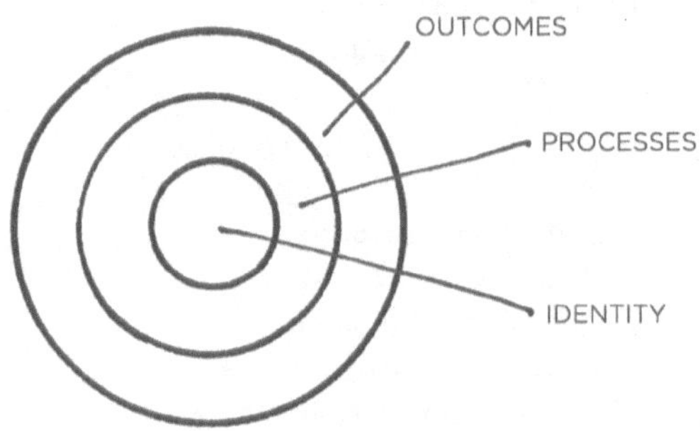

Outcome-based behaviour change is goal-driven like losing weight, publishing a book, or winning a championship. The second layer of processes is concerned with changing your habits to achieve a particular target and the third which is the most profound layer pertains to changing your identity. This means positive and progressive change in your core beliefs, self-image and judgments. According to James Clear, identity-based habits are long-lasting and productive vis-a-vis outcome-based habits. For instance, the goal should not be to read a book but to become a reader, similarly, the goal should not be to run a marathon but to become a runner or the goal should not be to learn an instrument rather

to become a musician. True change is actually a behaviour and an identity change. Perhaps the most interesting concept of this book is the habit loop.

Anything that you do and eventually want to develop into a habit has to go through four stages: cue, craving response, and reward. Cue is the trigger point that develops a craving in you to do something; just like the bell of your phone or notification on your phone. A response is usually followed by a reward which increases the probability of the act being repeated. As you perform an activity again and again the loop continues further, resultantly cementing that behaviour as a habit.

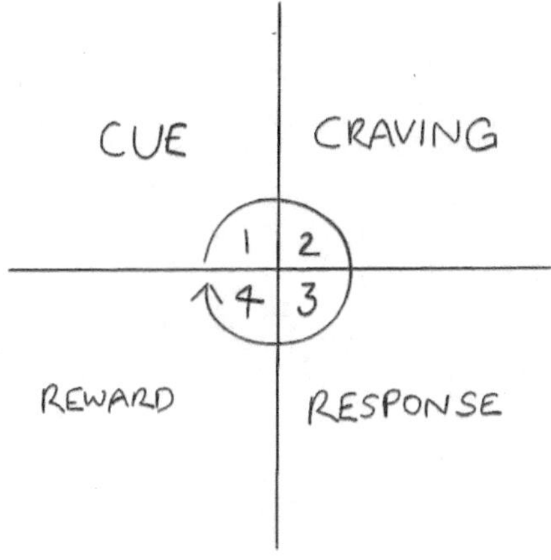

I am a very strong advocate of the fact that habits determine what will happen to us in the future. Therefore, if you want your future to be bright and prosperous, then reconstruct and realign your habits. Now promise me that as soon as you finish reading this summary you will work on two things: Adopt a good habit and destroy a bad one. Good luck!

I am a very strong advocate of the fact that habits determine what will happen to us in the future. Therefore, if you want your future to be bright and prosperous, then reconstruct and realign your habits.

PERSONAL NOTES

Use this space to write your notes and key takeaways from the book.

ALL
ANIMALS
ARE EQUAL,
BUT SOME
ANIMALS
ARE MORE
EQUAL THAN
OTHERS

ANIMAL FARM
Author: George Orwell
Genre: Fiction/Classics

Millions of books have been written in the last 2000 years of human history. While majority of them have been lost in oblivion, there are a few which have stood the test of time and have become immortal. The book which I will review in the coming few paragraphs can easily make it to the Top 100 books of all time. It is an absolute classic of English literature which, in such a succinct way, explores the deep layers of human behaviour and the way we politically conduct ourselves in society. It is a book that is valued across all cultures, groups, ethnicities and countries. Its famous statement "All animals are equal but some animals are more equal than others" has become part of common political jargon.

George Orwell's masterpiece "Animal Farm" catapulted him to fame and glory as a writer. There is hardly any book in English satire which can hold its ground in front of this magnum opus by Orwell. Satire can be generally described as the use of humour, irony, exaggeration or ridicule to expose and criticise people's stupidity or any wicked behaviour, particularly in the context of contemporary politics and other burning societal issues. It explores the negative aspects of society through humor so that feelings across the board are not hurt and the underlying message is precisely conveyed as well.

Before delving into the story of Animal Farm let me give you the background of this novel. George Orwell was a British author who, through Animal Farm, has tried to describe the political turmoil that existed in communist Russia during his time. He describes a rogue government that under the veil of equality becomes morally and financially corrupt. When struggling for power, it raises slogans of human rights, morality, equality and equity but as soon as it gains power, refutes and forgets all these virtues. The aspect which makes this novella stand out is the fact that Orwell has conveyed the message in the form of an allegory by personifying animals. Instead of directly talking about humans and their behaviours, he brings in animals and makes them do the talking. What a superb way of manifesting one's thought.

The story starts with a man named Mr. Jones who owns an animal farm. The farm has many kinds of animals like pigs, dogs, horses, sheep, chickens etc. All these animals are very unhappy with their owner, Mr. Jones, due to his oppressive and totalitarian nature. He has an unkind, miserly attitude that the animals absolutely abhor. One of those animals is a pig named Old Major who is highly idealistic and possesses leadership qualities. He is an expert in motivating his peers and inciting the animals to revolt. He tells them stories of self-rule and freedom, and convinces them to fight against the tyrant Mr. Jones so that they can establish their government. Eventually, all animals buy into his idea and rebel against Mr. Jones and chase him away. Although he tries to regain his farm but it continues to be ruled by the animals. Their unity becomes their biggest strength.

Once the war is finished there is a debate on the farm as to who will be the leader of the tribe and exercise control over the farm. By that time Old Major is dead. The competition eventually boils down to two pigs named Snowball and Napoleon. Napoleon is a cunning individual who, along with his accomplice Squealer, uses propaganda and deceit to evict Snowball from the farm and eventually becomes the leader of the farm.

As soon as he assumes power, he presents a charter to the animals which is quite impressive to look at. The best part of that charter is the last postulate which states "All Animals Are Equal." However, very soon Napoleon forgets all the morals that he had preached and spends his days enjoying the luxury of being the leader of the farm along with his friends. He makes all the animals toil hard each day without even providing them with adequate food.

One day, Napoleon orders all animals to build a windmill to generate electricity so that farm work can be made easier. Meanwhile, a nearby farmer named Frederick attacks the farm again but the animals, all together, defend themselves and protect the farm. During the same battle, Frederick's men destroy the newly built windmill. Moreover, a hard-working, loyal, diligent, and dedicated horse named Boxer (he epitomises the labour class who is naïve and always exploited) is also injured during the battle. Under the pretext of sending Boxer to the doctor, Napoleon slaughters him and pretends that the state tried to take care of him but he died a heroic death. After the battle, Napoleon makes changes in his charter and modifies his last postulate. This single line has become the identity of Animal Farm worldwide. It said, "All animals are equal but some animals are more equal than others."

The tyranny of Napoleon continues and all the animals have no option but to keep their heads down and obey him. Comparatively, the condition of the animals is even worse than it was at the time when Mr. Jones was in charge. Animals had rebelled against humans since they found them oppressive and mean without knowing that when they themselves will be in charge they will be stuck in the same quagmire of loot, corruption, moral bankruptcy and deceit.

Animals had rebelled against humans since they found them oppressive and mean without knowing that when they themselves will be in charge they will be stuck in the same quagmire of loot, corruption, moral bankruptcy and deceit.

Napoleon further cements his position by establishing a business partnership with the people he had rebelled against. The book concludes with a scene of a party in which Napoleon and his accomplices are having a great time along with their human business partners. All the animals are standing outside and

watching the entire scene unfold. They are clueless, helpless and disappointed. At the end of it all, there is no difference left between humans and animals.

Animal Farm is one of the most profound and thoughtful novels I have ever read. The underlying theme of the story is so meaningful and close to reality. If you dissect the characters in the story, you will realise that Mr. Jones represents the corrupt government of any country who is self-absorbed and doesn't care at all about common people. Old major who incited all the animals to revolt represents Karl Marx and his communist thought process which promotes rebellion against the powerful. Snowball represents an intelligent political worker. Napoleon represents a stubborn, clever and a cunning politician who promises but never delivers on his promises. Squealer acts as a propagandist in a totalitarian regime who always makes the people believe that all is going well despite all the atrocities. Boxer represents hard-working people who get caught up in the propaganda and sacrifice their lives for the country.

There are a number of riveting underlying themes behind the success of Animal Farm. One such theme is that of idealism which is manifested by Old Major who provokes the animals to revolt against the status quo in quest of setting up an ideal society based on equity and equality. Another theme is that of moral and financial corruption whereby things are promised by leaders but are never delivered to the public. Power corrupts and absolute power corrupts absolutely. Another theme is that of deception, propaganda, and exploitation. The leader brainwashes the public and makes them do the grunt work while enjoying the luxuries of power himself.

There is a lot of learning for all of us in Animal Farm. If we understand its deeply ingrained message, we can not only save ourselves from the tyrannical and selfish rulers but can protect and safeguard posterity as well.

PERSONAL NOTES

Use this space to write your notes and key takeaways from the book.

DON'T SAY I CAN'T AFFORD IT, RATHER SAY HOW CAN I AFFORD IT

RICH DAD POOR DAD

Author: Robert Kiyosaki
Genre: Self-help

Money is directly dovetailed to the fulfilment of desires in our lives. Back in the day, it was part of common folklore that money can't buy happiness but somehow my life experience totally negates this statement. Money can surely buy happiness, comfort and pleasures of life. Do not look at money as an evil outcome of the capitalistic society we live in today. Rather, view it as a medium through which you can fulfill your dreams. If you have an aspiration of buying a house, a good car, a watch, clothes, or going on a world tour, all of these dreams can only be fulfilled once you have money in your pocket. People at large tend to believe that fortune or wealth is determined by the luck of an individual; if he has been blessed by destiny, he will be rich. However, the reality is quite different. There is a definitive and objective formula, a secret recipe that is followed by people which makes them rich. There is a certain level of financial intelligence that people possess which leads to the accumulation of wealth and money.

A lot of literature has been written on how to make money, how to be rich, how to make a fortune but there are only a handful of books that have achieved the gold standard in terms of knowledge about wealth accumulation. One such book is "Rich Dad Poor Dad" by Robert Kiyosaki. Let's discuss what this book is all about. You never know- you can become a millionaire after reading the next few paragraphs.

Robert Kiyosaki is an American entrepreneur who wrote this book in the year 1997. In Rich Dad Poor Dad, he elaborated on the practices and most importantly the mindset which only a few people

possess that makes them rich. Since that time onwards, millions of its copies have been sold and the prime reason behind the book's success is that it teaches financial education in the easiest and simplest way. Though some of its concepts are quite controversial but despite that, the book is in great demand all over the world.

Robert Kiyosaki starts the book with a story of two fathers; one is his own and the other is his friend's father. His real father was a highly learned and educated individual holding a Ph.D degree. However, despite of all his academic achievements, he spent most of his life in poverty and scarcity. On the other hand, his friend's father could only make it to 8th grade but was super rich and financially stable. The difference in their financial status was primarily due to the mindset of both individuals. Robert's poor father always thought that money is the root of all mischief and all the evils in this world are due to money while his friend's rich father thought that not having money is the root of all mischief.

Whenever Robert's poor father would look at anything expensive, he always said, "I can't afford it, this is beyond my status." Whereas, whenever his friend's rich father came across something which was beyond his affordability he would say, "How can I afford this? What can I do to get it?" This thought process eventually guided him in becoming a man of fortune.

Robert's poor father always taught him to study hard, work hard and then hustle for a job to eventually become an employee. On the other hand, his friend's rich father always taught his son that you can never become rich by working for someone, so always think of setting up your own company and hiring people who can work for you.

The first lesson that Robert Kiyosaki teaches in

this book is that being rich has nothing to do with one's education. Man is not rich by his degree or qualification rather it is his mindset which makes him excel in life. If you are fixated on the thought of making money, then you will definitely make it. If you are a laggard and a procrastinator, then no matter what qualification you possess, you will never be able to make a fortune and be successful. This thought is somehow related to the law of attraction as well which states that if you are obsessed with something in life you will eventually get it.

The first lesson that Robert Kiyosaki teaches in this book is that being rich has nothing to do with one's education. Man is not rich by his degree or qualification rather it is his mindset which makes him excel in life.

Another very critical thing that Robert Kiyosaki advocates very strongly in this book is pertaining to the quintessential education system in which we teach everything but financial literacy. Students are taught theory instead of practical skills which will be the catalyst behind their professional success in life. The pedagogy of teaching and learning that is followed in our schools, colleges and universities is alien to the skills required to be successful in professional life. A great example of this concept is the Memon community of Karachi. Memons are mostly very rich due to their strong business sense. This sense of conducting business is neither taught to them in school nor at any university rather; they grow up with this financial literacy from childhood which eventually results in their financial success.

Another important tenet taught by Robert Kiyosaki in this book is called the "five-point rule of financial literacy." This rule is so simple that absolutely anyone can understand and make sense of it.

Its five aspects are:

- Income
- Expense
- Assets
- Liabilities
- Cash flow

Let's discuss these five points. Income is everything that you earn while expense is the money that you incur. Assets and liabilities are the two main concepts of this 5-point rule which you need to understand well because their explanation varies from the standard definition that is taught to commerce or accounting students.

Kiyosaki states that everything that puts money in your pocket is your asset and everything that takes money out of your pocket is your liability. This thought really shatters our traditional concepts pertaining to both. For instance, we think that buying real estate or a house is an asset but as per Kiyosaki since it took money out of our pocket it cannot be classified as an asset. It will only be classified as an asset when it starts earning for you. For example, putting your house, car or your real estate on rent.

Kiyosaki states that everything that puts money in your pocket is your asset and everything that takes money out of your pocket is your liability.

Rich people make assets while poor people spend their lives in managing liabilities. This one concept segregates the rich from the poor. Poor or middle-class people are always stuck in the vicious circle of managing their desires which never allows them to accumulate wealth.

Another important concept that Kiyosaki talks about is the "expense pattern" of any individual. Understand it from the following graph.

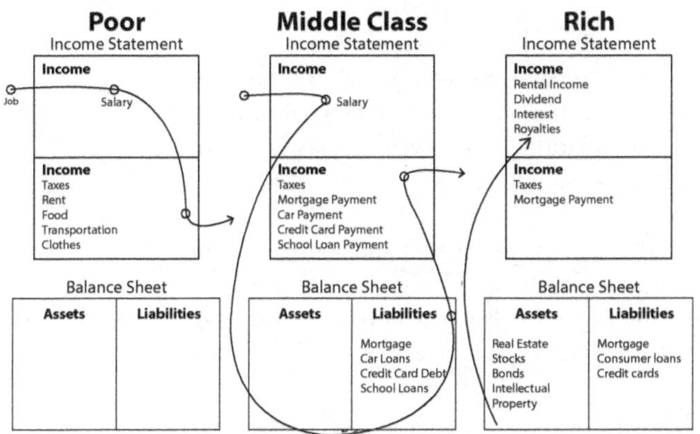

If you look at the expense pattern of poor people, you will see that as soon as they receive income it is immediately converted to expenditure. Middle class people spend their income first in paying off the liabilities like student, house or car loan and spend the remaining amount in balancing their expenses. This is the reason why they stay middle class. On the other hand, if you look at the expense pattern of rich people, as soon as they receive their income, they make assets. Whatever their expense is, they manage it from the income generated from those assets. That's the concept of "money makes money." This single practice makes people rich.

If you look at the expense pattern of rich people, as soon as they receive their income, they make assets. Whatever their expense is, they manage it from the income generated from those assets.

The controversial part of this book pertains to liabilities. Kiyosaki believes that taking money out of your pocket is a liability. Therefore, children too are a liability till the age they start earning money. Similarly, old people above the age of 60 are also a liability since they are no more contributors to the economy. It's inconceivable in our culture to think of children and parents as liabilities therefore, I do not agree with this concept. It might be true in the West but in our society, blood bonds are sacrosanct.

The best thing about this book is its stress on financial literacy which every individual should learn so that he can manage his cash flow of life efficiently and effectively. Now let me tell you a foolproof way of getting rich. Here you go:

Trait 1: You should always have the willingness to learn, unlearn and relearn. Always be ready in accepting something new. This will be your passport to the accumulation of knowledge, wisdom, and eventually becoming rich.

Trait 2: If you want to get rich and successful, you need to possess the hunger for growth. You need to have the fire in your belly to achieve something big. Your high ambitions and high energy will lead you to

make a fortune in your life.

Trait 3: You need to have strong perseverance, dedication and commitment. I have seen people with average intellect and talent becoming unbelievably rich and successful due to these traits.

Trait 4: Always be in pursuit of excellence. Whatever you do, try doing it to the best of your abilities. Practice and make yourself perfect in all your endeavours in life.

Trait 5: Implement the wondrous compound effect in your life. In a nutshell, compound effect states that if you continue to bring one percent improvement in your life on a daily basis, a day will come when you will move towards exponential growth whether it's about success, career or money.

Good luck!

You need to have strong perseverance, dedication and commitment. I have seen people with average intellect and talent becoming unbelievably rich and successful due to these traits.

In a nutshell, compound effect states that if you continue to bring one percent improvement in your life on a daily basis, a day will come when you will move towards exponential growth.

PERSONAL NOTES

Use this space to write your notes and key takeaways from the book.

LOLITA, THE LIGHT OF MY LIFE, FIRE OF MY LOINS. MY SIN, MY SOUL.

LOLITA
Author: Vladimir Nabokov
Genre: Fiction/Classics

A 37-year-old English professor is madly in love and obsessed with a 12-year-old girl named Dolores Haze whom he also calls Lolita. Not only is he in love with the little girl but is sexually attracted to her as well. This plot belongs to the cult classic novel written by Russian American writer Vladimir Nabokov titled "Lolita." When published in the year 1955, it took the world by storm due to its controversial theme revolving around pedophilia. Pedophilia is a psychiatric disorder in which an adult experiences sexual attraction towards children. These children are usually between the age of 9 and 13. When Vladimir Nabokov approached American publishers to publish his novel, they flatly refused. He eventually went to French publishers who agreed to publish it. Later on, countries like France and Australia banned the novel in their countries since it was talking about a topic that was considered taboo at that time.

Pedophilia is a psychiatric disorder in which an adult experiences sexual attraction towards children. These children are usually between the age of 9 and 13.

Lolita takes us on an emotional roller coaster ride with two main protagonists of the novel, an English professor named Humbert and a girl named Lolita. The professor develops feelings of love, lust and desire towards Dolores and the interaction between the two sets the stage for this remarkable book. Many agencies rate it as one of the finest works of literature of the 20th century. The phenomenal style of writing by Nabokov is breathtakingly fluid and profound. I classify it amongst the best novels I have read in my life, period. Let's move towards the storyline of the book.

The phenomenal style of writing by Nabokov is breathtakingly fluid and profound. I classify it amongst the best novels I have read in my life.

Professor Humbert during his childhood fell in love

with a girl named Annabel Leigh. He was 13 at that time and Annabel was 12. This love story ended prematurely when Annabel soon died of typhoid. Her death seriously dented Humbert psychologically. His unfulfilled love created a desire in him towards young girls whom he referred to as nymphets.

He tried to continue with his normal life and got married as well. However, it was a dysfunctional marriage and did not succeed. This made Humbert uncomfortable and he travelled to USA in search of better employment opportunities. He moves to a small town named Ramsdale where he starts residing in a house as a paying guest. The house is owned by a widow named Charlotte Haze. Although he doesn't like the house but the only reason that stops him there is the presence of a 12-year-old girl named Dolores, the daughter of Charlotte. He immediately falls for her beauty and innocence.

As time passes by, he not only falls head over heels in love with Dolores (who he refers to as Lolita) but gets sexually attracted to her as well. He tries to get close to her physically through the smallest of contacts but never really gets hold of her. In the meantime, Charlotte has developed feelings for Humbert and proposes to him by giving him two options. Either he is to marry her or leave the house. Humbert is stuck between the devil and the deep blue sea since the center of gravity of his life was Dolores and he couldn't afford not living close to her. Therefore, he had no option but to accept the proposal by Charlotte.

Like his previous marriage, this was a dysfunctional marriage since Humbert had no emotions for Charlotte. In order to vent out his emotions, he used to write a diary in which he explicitly expressed his feelings for Lolita. One day this diary falls into the hands of Charlotte and she is absolutely devastated by what she reads. She confronts Humbert and both have

In order to vent out his emotions, he used to write a diary in which he explicitly expressed his feelings for Lolita.

a venomous argument. In complete rage, Charlotte rushes out of the house and dies in a car accident.

Dolores at that time was at a summer camp. Humbert immediately goes to meet Dolores and informs her that her mother is ill and hospitalised. He takes her to a high-end hotel and tries to rape her after giving her a sedative, but the pill doesn't work. In the morning, Dolores reveals to him that she has already lost her virginity by having sexual intercourse with a boy at the camp. This makes Humbert furious and he takes it as a justification to abuse her and rape her. He finally informs her of her mother's death as well.

Humbert and Dolores start travelling across the country from one city to another. During this time, Humbert feels that someone is following them. Finally, they settle in Beardsley where Humbert adopts the role of her father and gets her enrolled in a local school. During all this time, he tries to bribe Dolores in exchange for sexual favours. One day, Dolores falls sick and is admitted to a hospital. She is discharged from the hospital one night by her uncle. As soon as Humbert finds this out, he becomes frenetic since he knows she doesn't have any relatives and acquaintances. His doubt that someone is following them is confirmed. That person is Clare Quilty, a friend of Charlotte and a famous playwright.

For the next two years, Humbert keeps searching for Dolores. One day, he receives a letter from her in which she has written that she is pregnant and is in immediate need of money. Humbert grabs a gun and immediately traces her whereabouts. Upon meeting her, she informs Humbert that she loved Quilty but he left her when she rejected starring in one of his pornographic films. All this makes Humbert furious with anger. He traces Quilty and shoots him down. The police catch Humbert and put him behind bars.

The entire story of Dolores (Lolita) is penned down by him as a memoir during his stay at the jail. He also writes that his memoir should not be published until Lolita is alive. Lolita eventually dies young at the age of 22.

That's the storyline of this masterpiece. The rhythm of words, the articulation of human emotions, and the engaging juggernaut of the plot make it an extraordinary read. It is a work of genius. Have a look at the crispness, vitality, and intensity of the opening lines (mentioned below) of the novel which set the stage for the entire plot.

Lolita, the light of my life, fire of my loins. My sin, my soul. Lo-lee-ta: the tip of the tongue taking a trip of three steps down the palate to tap, a three, on the teeth. Lo. Lee. Ta. She was Lo, plain Lo, in the morning, standing four feet ten in one sock. She was Lola in slacks. She was Dolly at school. She was Dolores on the dotted line. But in my arms, she was always Lolita.

The quality of writing makes Lolita an indispensable read and one of the best pieces of English literature.

The entire story of Dolores (Lolita) is penned down by him as a memoir during his stay at the jail. He also writes that his memoir should not be published until the time Lolita is alive.

The rhythm of words, the articulation of human emotions, and the engaging juggernaut of the plot make it an extraordinary read. It is a work of genius.

PERSONAL NOTES

Use this space to write your notes and key takeaways from the book.

A DEVASTATING INDICTMENT OF WOMEN'S ROLE IN MUSLIM SOCIETY

MY FEUDAL LORD
Author: Tehmina Durrani
Genre: Autobiography

Mostly an author publishes his/her book to convey a message, to share a point of view, or to disseminate any information. Normally, whenever a book is published, its author is usually appreciated and encouraged, specially by his near and dear ones. However, the book that I am about to review is different. When the author published this book, she had to face fourteen years of enmity from her friends, family and even her parents. That's really a hard price to pay to speak your heart out. When Tehmina Durrani published "My Feudal Lord" in the year 1991, it created an absolute turmoil in the political landscape of Pakistan. It is one of the most riveting and interesting books written by a Pakistani author. There are very few pieces of literature that keep the reader glued from the start to the finish; My Feudal Lord is one such book.

When Tehmina Durrani published "My Feudal Lord" in the year 1991, it created an absolute turmoil in the political landscape of Pakistan. It is one of the most riveting and interesting books written by a Pakistani author.

The basic theme of the book revolves around male chauvinism, patriarchy, feudalism and infidelity. Never before has someone spoken so boldly and fearlessly against the feudal lords and the system of male dominance in Pakistan, especially in politics. Tehmina Durrani dared to speak up against the atrocities that she had to face in her life which struck a chord with the audience. That is the reason which made My Feudal Lord such a runaway success. Let's review the background of the book.

The basic theme of the book revolves around male chauvinism, patriarchy, feudalism, and infideltity. Never before has someone spoken so boldly and fearlessly against the feudal lords and the system of male dominance in Pakistan especially in politics.

Tehmina Durrani is the current wife of Shahbaz Sharif. She was previously married to Ghulam Mustafa Khar (Former Chief Minister and Governor of Punjab). Khar was regarded as the most powerful minister in the history of the Punjab government,

which is the reason why he got the title of "Sher-e-Punjab" as well. He was the founding member of Pakistan People's Party and a close confidant of Zulfiqar Ali Bhutto. Tehmina Durrani was his fourth wife. The context of My Feudal Lord revolves around the fourteen years of marriage between the two. It's a breathtaking story of their pre-marital romantic entanglement, the life after marriage and the devastating domestic violence she faced as Khar's wife.

It's a breathtaking story of their pre-marital romantic entanglement, the life after marriage and the devastating domestic violence she faced during that time.

Tehmina Durrani belonged to an affluent background but her childhood was very disturbing. One of the aspects which contributed towards her emotional imbalance was the behaviour of her mother. She states in the book that her mother used to hate her for her skin tone which was wheatish. It's unimaginable to think of the mental turmoil a child goes through when your own mother discriminates against you to a point where she starts hating you. She has given a very vivid account of her childhood, her privileges, weaknesses and insecurities. Eventually, when she grew up, she married a man named Anees Khan with whom she had a daughter. While married to Khan, she met Ghulam Mustafa Khar and subsequently love started blossoming between the two. She has been very open and transparent in the book and hasn't played the victim card. She has openly accepted her infidelity in her first marriage and the sexual closeness she enjoyed before marrying Ghulam Mustafa Khar. It takes courage for a woman in our country to be so upright and ruthlessly honest.

She states in the book that her mother used to hate her for the colour of her skin which was wheatish. It's unimaginable to think of the mental turmoil a child goes through when your own mother discriminates against you to a point where she starts hating you.

The way she has explained her initial romance with Khar remains the highlight of the book. The story where she has elucidated the intimacy between herself and Khar is backed by the most smooth and appropriate choice of words. The rhythm of her language makes the reader feel as if you are reading Emily Bronte or Jane Austin's work.

She writes that the first two years of her marriage were full of love, affection and devotion but soon things started to crumble. She elaborates that Mustafa Khar deep inside was an insecure male chauvinist who was driven by the desire to control women owing to his feudal background. She had to face terrible verbal and physical abuse from him. When you read the description of the grotesque physical violence done by Khar on her you can envision what Tehmina Durrani must have gone through. Kudos to the tolerance, restraint and patience she showed during her abusive marriage with Mr. Khar.

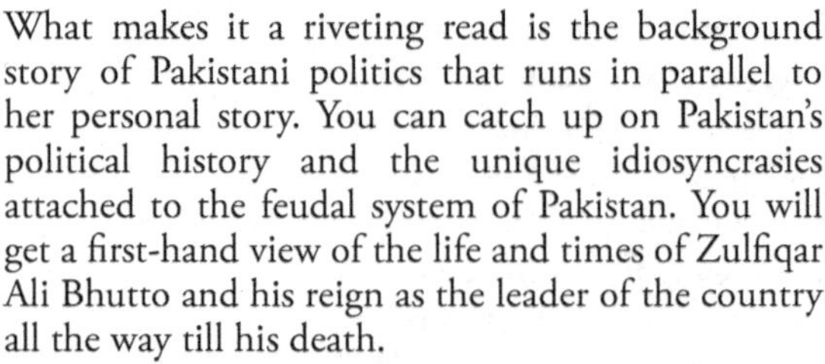

She elaborates that Mustafa Khar deep inside was an insecure male chauvinist who was driven by the desire to control women owing to his feudal background.

What makes it a riveting read is the background story of Pakistani politics that runs in parallel to her personal story. You can catch up on Pakistan's political history and the unique idiosyncrasies attached to the feudal system of Pakistan. You will get a first-hand view of the life and times of Zulfiqar Ali Bhutto and his reign as the leader of the country all the way till his death.

Tehmina Durrani had an absolutely no holds barred approach while writing this book. She even exposed the illegitimate affair between her husband, Mr. Khar and her sister. Through her writing, she has shown Mustafa Khar as a quintessential WADERA (Feudal) of Pakistan who is intoxicated with his power. She writes that like most of the feudals, Mr. Khar believed that the sole purpose for the existence of women is to please men. He has several shades in his personality which you will understand only when you read the book.

She has vividly depicted the plight of women in our country who are merely treated as slaves and considered the lesser gender. No book has highlighted patriarchal domination the way My Feudal Lord has. The oppression that women face in our country is usually brushed under the carpet and ignored. Society tends to stigmatise women who have the courage to speak up against the atrocities that they face. This is where My Feudal Lord strikes a chord since it empowers the voice of women who are threatened by the double standards of society.

YOU

ARE THE

MASTER

OF YOUR

DESTINY

THINK AND GROW RICH

Author: Napoleon Hill
Genre: Self-help

Napoleon Hill is a very famous author who, in the year 1937, wrote a masterpiece that became the gold standard in the genre of self-help and motivational books. It is titled "Think and Grow Rich." This book is a result of twenty-five years of research and hard work in which Napoleon Hill interviewed 25,000 people in the quest to seek an answer to one question, "What makes people rich?" Finally, after years of perseverance and dedication, he was able to crack the code and found the secret formula through which people can become rich and prosperous. He consolidated his research in the form of this book so that people have a sure shot formula in front of them to get rich.

Napoleon Hill has elaborated 13 principles that contribute towards making an individual successful. Here are all 13.

1. Desire – The urge to achieve something.
2. Faith – Complete trust and confidence.
3. Specialised Knowledge – Profound knowledge of a specific discipline.
4. Imagination – The ability to think.
5. Sixth Sense – Strong intuition.
6. Persistence – Strong dedication towards a cause.
7. Auto Suggestion – The medium for influencing the subconscious mind.
8. Subconscious Mind – Bridge between finite mind and infinite intelligence.
9. Sex Transmutation – Channeling of carnal desires.
10. The Brain – Seat of intelligence.
11. Organised Planning – Definite and practical

plan of action.

12. Decision Making – Quick and selection.
13. Power of Master Mind – Alliance of individuals with different strengths.

Let's narrow down on some of the key points that make this book such an awesome read.

Napoleon Hill has suggested that to be rich and prosperous in life, it is absolutely indispensable to have a desire to accumulate wealth. This means that you need to have a strong urge and hunger to earn money instead of just flowing with the tide of life. He reiterates this tenet of desire time and again in the book and suggests that whatever you are in pursuit of in your life, desire to achieve it will be your main anchor. Desire directly correlates to possessing fire in the belly and the hunger to achieve any possible ambition in your life. Once you have the desire to earn money you need to follow this six-step process.

1. Write on a piece of paper or in your diary the amount of money you want to earn. For instance, it can be 1 Lakh, 10 Lakh, 10 Crores.
2. How much are you willing to sacrifice and struggle in your life to earn this money.
3. This plan has to be time-barred and needs to be given a due date. For instance, you can write "I want to earn 10 Lakh by the end of the year 2023."
4. You need to form an action plan to earn this amount. What you intend to do and what you need to do to earn this amount. It can be multiple income streams, investments, business, etc.
5. Combine the first four points and make a statement. This statement will govern your movement in life. For instance, it will look something like this, "I need to earn 10 Lakh Rupees by the end of the year 2023 from my own business and I am willing to work 16 hours a day to accomplish this."

6. Read this statement out aloud to yourself every day.

Superficially, these six steps look easy to execute. If it was that simple every individual would have been a millionaire today. However, these six steps are closely connected to the "Law of Attraction" whereby we tend to attract everything in the universe our way if we think about it and want it badly. Do try to make these six steps part of your life. You never know, you can be on your way to earn fortunes in life. If you ask my personal opinion, I have tested this and it works with almost 90% accuracy. The only thing you need to keep in the back of the mind is that results will not be overnight; you will have to persevere and stay committed over a long period of time.

Another very important thing that Napoleon Hill discusses in this book is faith and the subconscious mind. He elaborates that the individual who has faith in his abilities, competence and skills has more probability of earning and getting rich. This faith is dovetailed to your subconscious mind which drives your thought. As they say that both poverty and riches are offspring of your thought. If you have confidence in your capabilities and can tame your mind to think positively then you can increase your chances of becoming rich. An optimistic mind leads to prosperity while a pessimistic thought process leads to adversity and scarcity.

The highlight of the book is Napoleon's perspective about Knowledge. He says that there are two types of knowledge; one is general and the other is Specialised. He derides general knowledge and advocates the pursuit of Specialised knowledge since it acts as a catalyst when you are on the hunt for wealth. He quotes examples of Thomas Edison, the great inventor, whereby he only had three months of formal schooling. Similarly, Henry Ford, the greatest entrepreneur, also had limited education. What he is trying to convey is

that Specialised, practical and pragmatic knowledge in any discipline of your life will set you up for success instead of rote learning and theory.

There is another controversial subject that Napoleon Hill alludes to in this book and that is about the mystery of Sex Transmutation. What he actually means is that the greatest drive which titillates a man is sexual desire. If this desire is channelised and transmuted it can lead to enhanced imagination, courage, persistence, willpower and refined creative ability leading to the accumulation of wealth and fortune.

When you would want to implement these strategies in your life there will be inhibitions, apprehension and reluctance. Napoleon Hill regards them as six ghosts of fear. These ghosts are the biggest impediments in an individual's pursuit towards riches. These are the fear of poverty, the fear of criticism, the fear of ill health, the fear of loss of love, the fear of old age and the fear of death. Once overcome, the path ahead is crystal clear.

PERSONAL NOTES

Use this space to write your notes and key takeaways from the book.

SUCCESS DEMANDS WAKING UP EARLY AND MAKING IT COUNT

THE 5 AM CLUB
Author: Robin Sharma
Genre: Self-help

Getting up early in the morning seems to be the biggest challenge for a majority of people. They find it really hard to muster the motivation to rise early and get on with life in full zeal and zest. I see not waking up early morning as the single biggest impediment to the growth and success of an individual. This is because waking up at dawn holds miraculous powers which can nurture your mind and body, and boost your creativity and productivity in life. Early risers tend to be several steps ahead of the pack which acts as a big catalyst in their prosperity in life. Whether it is Barack Obama (former president of USA), Indra Nooyi (former CEO of Pepsi), Elon Musk (Founder of PayPal, Tesla and SpaceX), or Tim Cook (CEO of Apple); all these individuals make the best of their mornings to lead a successful life. One of the secrets behind their success is waking up at 5 am every day.

What's the magic of waking up at 5 am? What powers do early mornings hold for us? What can we do to boost our productivity early morning? How can we wake up at 5 am? All these questions will be answered in the next few paragraphs as I dissect a famous book written by a stalwart of the self-help genre, Robin Sharma, titled "The 5 AM Club". This entire book is dedicated to making your early mornings magical; so let's delve into it.

Robin Sharma insists that people who do big things in life and are super successful are not products of their destiny or fate. These individuals deviate from the norm and are eccentric enough to choose a path that has not been trodden on before. They execute things that majority of the people even fail to think

of which in turn leads to greater rewards in life. If you think that you can achieve the same prosperity in life by waking up later in the day when half of the day is gone, then you need to recalibrate your thinking. One of the facets of progress is directly dovetailed to the time you wake up at. If you are an early riser, you will surely reap the benefits of this routine. However, if you start waking up at 5 am and develop it into a habit then you simply become unstoppable.

Sharma writes that the hour between 5am to 6am is the victory hour. In these 60 minutes, you can perform several activities which can nurture your personality spiritually, mentally and physically. The activities that you perform in this one-hour cater to the following.

1. Mindset – The ability to be optimistic and think positively
2. Heartset – How you regulate your positive and negative emotions
3. Soulset – Your spirituality
4. Healthset – How healthy you are mentally and physically

Now let's address the elephant in the room and seek to answer the following question: "How can we

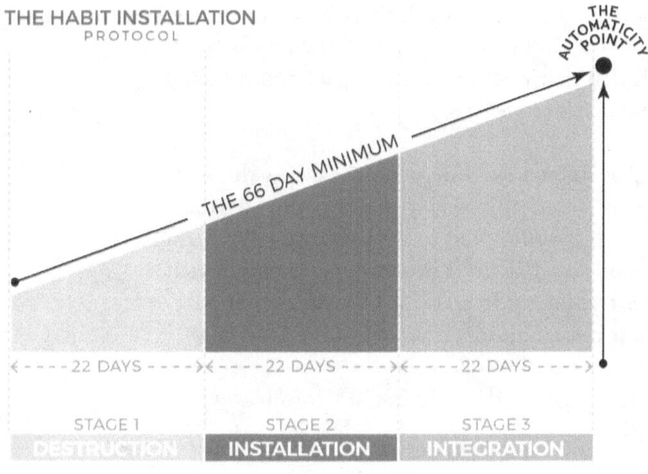

develop the habit of waking up at 5 am." Sharma states a step-by-step approach in the book which you can follow to gradually nurture this habit and make it an integral part of your life. He labels it as the "Sixty-Six Days Formula". He has divided these sixty-six days into three equal portions of 22 days each as you can see from the preceding diagram.

Sharma states a step-by-step approach in the book which you can follow to gradually nurture this habit and make it an integral part of your life. He labels it as the "Sixty-Six Days Formula."

Stage 1 is known as "Destruction". These are the 22 days in which you have to destroy your bad habits and your existing mental pattern. Identify the sequence of your life and write down all the negative habits that you have made part of your personality. In this phase of destruction, start dismantling them one after the other. In the initial few days, it will be relatively easy for you since you are motivated and all gung-ho about it but as you move along and days pass, you need to keep yourself focused and committed to the cause. This will require serious soul searching and constant reinforcement of motivation.

In the initial few days, it will be relatively easy for you since you are motivated and all gung-ho about it but as you move along and days pass, you need to keep yourself focused and committed to the cause.

Stage 2 is known as the "Installation" phase. This, as per my personal experience, is the most difficult of all the 3 stages. This is because as days pass by you start to question yourself as to why am I doing all this? What's the need of taking so much pain? You feel like giving up on a few days, but that is where you have to stay steadfast. This is because in these 22 days you have to actually install the new habit in your life so that it stays there for good and becomes part of your lifestyle.

Stage 3 is known as "Integration". This is the stage when the new habit slowly starts taking its roots inside you. If you intend to start waking up at 5 am then at this stage it starts becoming easy and in fact, you start enjoying it as well. Hitting the "snooze" button is not an option anymore.

Now let's review the "20:20:20" formula which

refers to the activities that you need to perform from 5 to 6 am (victory hour). In the first 20 minutes, you need to exercise or do any physical exertion. It can be going to the gym, doing yoga or having a brisk walk in the park. It has to be a high-intensity workout so that you sweat and encourage the release of Dopamine and discourage the intensity of Cortisol. Dopamine is a neurotransmitter that boosts our motivation and happiness while Cortisol stunts our growth and snubs the genius inside us.

The next 20 minutes belong to meditation. It can be in any form. The aim is to bolster your focus and provide catharsis to your soul. This spiritual exercise of 20 minutes will go a long way in keeping you balanced and in harmony with your environment. You can also use this time to contemplate important things in your life and plan your day ahead.

In the last 20 minutes, you have to invest in yourself by enhancing your learning capability. It can be done through reading a book, listening to audio books, watching a motivational video or learning a new skill. When all these three core activities combine in this victory hour, you will witness extraordinary results which can be life-changing. I can give you my personal guarantee that this really works.

I strongly urge all of you to make waking up early an integral part of your life. Do not waste your hours in sleeping through the day. It's detrimental to your progress in life and numbs your mind. Fight your demons and enjoy the morning sunlight and make each day count.

PERSONAL NOTES

Use this space to write your notes and key takeaways from the book.

MY 100
OFF 37
BALLS
CHANGED
MY LIFE
UPSIDE
DOWN

GAME CHANGER
Author: Shahid Afridi
Genre: Autobiography

October 4, 1996, is a historical day for the game of cricket. It was a day when a young teenage cricketer from Pakistan named Shahid Afridi scored the fastest century in the history of One Day International cricket. This was his ticket to fame and fortune after which he never looked back. Shahid Afridi became an overnight star and the most sought-after celebrity in the world of cricket. Though he sometimes invited the ire of the people due to his swashbuckling style of play, yet "Boom Boom" (as he is famously known) has continued to entertain people over the course of the past three decades.

A couple of years ago, he wrote his autobiography titled "Game Changer." It is a story of his life in which he has written about his struggle, his time playing cricket for Pakistan and the associated controversies. It is quite inspirational as well for youngsters who aspire to be cricketers or who in general seek motivation from the life history of famous celebrities. The book has been co-written by himself and Wajahat Saeed Khan, who is a journalist. Although the book does not follow a quintessential sequence of an autobiography yet it keeps the reader glued to the content. Let's delve into the life of Shahid Afridi.

Shahid Afridi is a Pakhtun who originally hails from Khyber Pakhtunkhwa. However, he has spent most of his life in Karachi. He comes from a humble background whereby his father was a small businessman and they were a family of eleven siblings. During his childhood, he took to the streets of Karachi, passionately playing cricket. He writes

that he was absolutely obsessed with playing cricket and could spend hours and hours bowling and batting.

During this time his father's fortunes came crashing down as he had to face a huge monetary loss due to his investments in the stock market. He recounts very vividly those moments when his family was undergoing sheer financial turmoil. He has first-hand experience of the time when you are broke and the family is hardly able to survive. It was at this time of adversity that he decided that, come what may, he will be a professional cricketer one day since that was the only thing that interested him in life and had the power to salvage his family.

Finally, he got the chance to play for Pakistan in the year 1996 and in just his second ODI he achieved the monumental feat of the fastest century. What followed was a roller coaster ride of hits and misses. Sometimes he faltered and sometimes he won the hearts of the audience through his hard-hitting. One thing I must appreciate is that he has been very candidly honest in the book. He has acknowledged the fact that he was the most most inconsistent player in the team and the reason behind this inconsistency is actually his fastest innings.

Afridi admits that he was in reality a bowler who could bat a bit. However, as soon as he got the fastest hundred, people started having huge expectations from him. Every time he went out to bat the crowd was chanting and ranting for the sixes. This made him a bit confused. He also admits to the fact that during his hard and confusing times, no one coached or mentored him except Bob Wolmer. He holds him in high regard.

What stands out in the book are his controversial statements against the legends of Pakistan cricket like Javed Miandad and Waqar Younis. He states that

Javed Miandad is a legendary player but deep inside he possesses a very weak personality. He has a sense of entitlement about himself and wants everyone to follow his instructions. Instead of leading through competence, he demands respect and still feels that he is part of the playing eleven instead of acting as a coach or a mentor. He quotes one incident when in his 2nd test at Chennai he scored a century against India. Initially, Miandad strongly opposed his induction into the team and it was only because of Wasim Akram that he got the opportunity to play. Just before the post-match presentation, he spoke to him and said that when you are asked questions about your performance today, mention my name as the catalyst behind this brilliant performance. Afridi writes that Miandad's credibility hit rock bottom at that time and he came across as a man of low stature.

With respect to Waqar Younis, he says that he was a below-average captain and a disastrous coach. He lacks the leadership qualities and is an absolute micro manager who doesn't even let his players breathe freely. On the contrary, he is all praises for Wasim Akram. He considers him a big brother and his staunch supporter. He proclaims that after Imran Khan, Wasim Akram was the only player who had refined leadership qualities and who mentored him. No wonder Wasim Akram has written the foreword of this book as well.

Afridi has revealed the dirty side of Pakistani cricket as well, where it is brimming with team politics, nepotism and match-fixing. He writes about the fragile egos of leading cricketers and how they are not nurtured enough to operate at an international level.

He also reveals his opinions about leading political figures like Imran Khan, Bilawal and Nawaz Sharif. He quotes an incident when during his fallout with Ijaz Butt (Former Chairman PCB), Bilawal offered arbitration in exchange for participation in his rallies in Larkana and other areas of Sindh. He also writes that Bilawal Bhutto is just a superficial face of Pakistan People's Party, with strings in reality being pulled by Asif Ali Zardari who runs the show. He has admitted his love for Imran Khan as a cricketer but is skeptical about his performance as a politician. Afridi believes that the people around Mr. Khan are not able enough and mostly are renegades from other parties who have never done anything good for the country.

With respect to Nawaz Sharif, he says that no matter what allegations of corruption he has on himself, the gentleman knows how to deliver. He talks about all provincial capitals in the country and picks Lahore as the best one, attributing its prosperity to Mr. Sharif. He is all praises for the Pakistan Army as well but doesn't like their intrusion in national politics.

He also lets the readers in on his personal life and talks about his relationship with females during his heydays. Quoting one such incident, he states that once he started talking to a girl who had a very beautiful voice. Eventually, after a few months of talking on the phone, they decided to meet up on Eid day. As soon as he opened the door to greet her, a fourteen-year-old boy was standing at the door. The boy had been fooling him for months in the disguise of a lady.

He also reveals the secret of the bat which he used to strike the fastest 100. That bat actually belonged to the great Sachin Tendulkar. What happened was that Tendulkar had given this bat to Waqar Younis so he could get an exact replica developed from Sialkot (Sialkot is a city in Pakistan that produces the best sports equipment in the world). On the way back, the team was stopping in Nairobi to play a few ODIs. It was during this time that Waqar Younis gave that bat to Shahid Afridi. The rest as they say is history.

Shahid Afridi is a very confident, transparent and open individual. He doesn't shy away from speaking his heart out and that is what he has done in his book. He is one of the few superstars of Pakistan who can drive an audience to the stadium. Keeping a close look at his demeanor these days, I prophesize that he will venture into politics someday. Maybe we will have a second Prime Minister with a cricket background. Let's see.

PERSONAL NOTES
Use this space to write your notes and key takeaways from the book.

PERSONAL NOTES

Use this space to write your notes and key takeaways from the book.

WHEN YOU WANT SOMETHING FROM ALL YOUR HEART, THE WHOLE UNIVERSE CONSPIRES IN HELPING YOU TO ACHIEVE IT

THE ALCHEMIST
Author: Paulo Coelho
Genre: Fiction/Motivational

Paulo Coelho is a Brazilian author who rose to international fame courtesy of his cult classic "The Alchemist." Published in 1988, it instantly became an international bestseller and has been translated into dozens of languages, selling millions of copies across the globe. It is a transformational book which takes you on a journey of self-discovery and enlightenment. Each and every paragraph of this book is thought-provoking and remarkable. It is a story of a boy named Santiago who embarks on a life-changing journey in pursuit of his dreams. The writing is so simple, yet powerful that as you progress through the novel you tend to see yourself in Santiago and experience his breathtaking journey. Let's find out what makes The Alchemist such a life-changing book.

Once upon a time in Andalusia, Spain there lived a boy named Santiago. He loved to travel so he requested his father to give him some goats which he would rear to different villages. A few months prior he had met a lovely girl in a city named Tarifa, so he decided to visit the place again and meet her. The journey towards the city was long. While he was on his way to the city the day slowly transformed into dusk and eventually night. He thought of taking an overnight rest and slept under a Sycamore tree close to an old church.

During his sleep, he witnessed a dream in which a child starts playing with his goats and holds his fingers, leading him to the pyramids of Egypt. When he reaches the pyramids, he informs him that there is a treasure buried around here but as he is about to tell its exact location, Santiago wakes up. He gets a little upset since he has seen this dream several times now. This time he intends to find out its essence and for this, he visits a woman in Tarifa who is a master in interpreting dreams.

The woman says that she will let him know the meaning of this dream but she wants a 1/10th share of the treasure once he gets it. Santiago eagerly agrees to her demand. The woman lets him know that he has a great treasure written in his destiny but in order to get to it, he needs to travel to Egypt. Santiago is left perplexed and doesn't believe in what the woman just said. He steps out of her home and meets an old man on the street who also starts referring to the same treasure that the woman just spoke about. Santiago thinks that the woman must have told the old man about the treasure and considers it an act of treachery on her part. Just then the old man writes the name of Santiago's parents on the ground and tells him some of his personal secrets. Santiago is left in a state of shock to hear his own personal secrets which no one knows of. The old man apprises him that he can tell the location of the treasure but on one condition that Santiago will have to give him 1/10th of his goats, to which he agrees. This is when the old man utters some beautiful lines.

He says that when a person is young, his dreams, goals and objectives are big. However, as he grows up he starts forgetting about his dreams due to undue pressure of society, peers and the environment. A time comes when he absolutely forgets all that he had dreamt of and starts spending an average life. When you want something badly the whole universe conspires in helping you to achieve it.

He finally convinces Santiago to sell his goats and give 1/10th of the amount to the old man. In exchange, he gives Santiago two stones that he can use to understand the signs of nature and make the best decisions. Santiago decides to go in pursuit of the treasure and first reaches Tangiers, a city in Morocco. As soon as he reaches there, robbers attack him and snatch all his money. Goats are gone, money is gone, the house is gone and he is alone in an unknown country. However, Santiago is a fighter and doesn't give up. He finds himself a job in a crystal shop where in exchange for two loaves of bread he will shine and clean the crystals so that their probability of selling increases.

The presence of Santiago turns the tables for the crystal shop. It starts attracting a lot of customers leading to a significant increase in sales. The owner becomes very happy with Santiago and starts offering him money as well. Within six months, Santiago accumulates a lot of money which is good enough to sponsor his trip to the pyramids. One day he finds out that a caravan is going from Morocco to Egypt via the Sahara Desert and he decides to join them. In the caravan, he meets an Englishman who tells him that he is in search of an alchemist whose age is 250 years and who knows how to turn copper into gold.

As the two approach the Alchemist's village, a brawl breaks out between two tribes and therefore they decide to stay in the village for a few days before continuing their journey. There Santiago meets a girl named Fatima. He falls head over heels in love with her and they start spending time together. One fine day Santiago sees two eagles grappling in the sky. Understanding it as a sign of nature, Santiago quickly visits the village chief and prophesizes that their village is about to be attacked.

His prophecy comes true and since the village people were prepared, they easily defeated the approaching army. The village chief is delighted and showers

Santiago with a lot of money along with making him the village councillor. A thought comes to his mind that now he has all the money he wants, he has a house, he holds a good position and he has Fatima as well then why does he need to pursue his dream any further. He lets Fatima in on his thoughts who doesn't agree with him and persuades him to continue with his journey to the pyramids.

Santiago and the Alchemist set out in search of the treasure in the Pyramids. During the journey, a few tribesmen think that they are spies; they snatch their money and take them into custody. The Alchemist plays a masterstroke here, he tells the village chief that this boy Santiago is a magician and if you do not let him continue on his journey, he will summon a desert storm which will blow away your entire village. The chief laughs at this and says that if that is true, I'll let you go and if not, then I'll kill both of you.

Santiago really gets upset with the Alchemist and questions his nonsense. In response, the Alchemist tells Santiago that these three days are an opportunity to save our lives, so put aside the fear of life and death, become harmonious with the system of nature and understand the language of the desert. On the third day, in reality, strong winds start blowing and fearing for their life, the tribesmen let the two of them go.

The Alchemist and Santiago stop at a monk's hut on the way. There the Alchemist first turns copper into gold and divides the gold into four parts. The first part is given to Santiago, the second part is given to the monk, the third part he keeps himself and the fourth part is given to the monk again. He says that when Santiago is back from the pyramids, he has to give him this piece of gold. As soon as he says that, the Alchemist disappears. Santiago continues his journey to his destination alone and finally reaches

A thought comes to his mind that now he has all the money he wants, he has a house, he holds a good position and he has Fatima as well then why does he need to pursue his dream any further.

The alchemist tells Santiago that these three days are an opportunity to save our lives, so put aside the fear of life and death and become harmonious with the system of nature and understand the language of the desert.

the pyramids. As soon as he starts digging for the treasure, thieves show up and start beating Santiago thinking that he has a lot of gold in his possession.

Santiago lets them in on his dream; to which they start laughing. The head of the thieves informs him that he also saw a dream in which there is an old church near Tarifa, outside the church is a Sycamore tree and hidden under the tree is a great treasure. He adds that I am not a foolish moron like you who struggles so hard to pursue his dream. They call him insane and leave him there alone. Santiago smiles and knows where the treasure is.

The head of the thieves informs him that he also saw a dream in which there is an old church near Tarifa, outside the church is a Sycamore tree and under the tree is hidden a great treasure. He adds that I am not a foolish moron like you who struggles so hard to pursue his dream.

This was the story of Santiago which has inspired millions and millions of people over the years. Let me mention a few key takeaways from his story.

1. Always dare to dream. Your life should be driven by a purpose. That purpose should instill in you the urge to work hard and strive perennially in life.
2. Be steadfast and adamant. The journey of life is laced with hard work, failure, stress, frustration, agony and happiness. You will face innumerable hurdles and obstacles along the way. If you persevere, success will be yours.
3. Never be complacent. Once you achieve a mark or fulfill your dream, never settle down. There is always a new challenge ahead. It happened twice in the story when Santiago could have settled down. One was when he was working in the crystal shop and the second time when he was offered councillorship in the village, but he kept moving ahead. Realisation of your objective should be an opportunity for pursuing new ventures
4. Choose your life partner wisely. In the story, Fatima plays a perfect role of a supporting and loving partner. She is willing to sacrifice her

Choose your life partner wisely. In the story, Fatima plays a perfect role of a supporting and loving partner. She is willing to sacrifice her time so that Santiago can go ahead and fulfill his dream.

time so that Santiago can go ahead and fulfill his dream. She doesn't stop him in his strides rather acts as an agent of positive change. I have seen people getting destroyed after marriage having chosen the wrong partner.

The Alchemist has inspired umpteen number of people to achieve big. I urge you to be the Santiago of your life and relentlessly pursue whatever you want in life.

PERSONAL NOTES

Use this space to write your notes and key takeaways from the book.

IF YOU WANT
PEOPLE
TO BE
INTERESTED
IN YOU, THEN
YOU HAVE
TO BE
INTERESTED
IN PEOPLE

HOW TO WIN FRIENDS & INFLUENCE PEOPLE
Author: Dale Carnegie
Genre: Self-help/Motivational

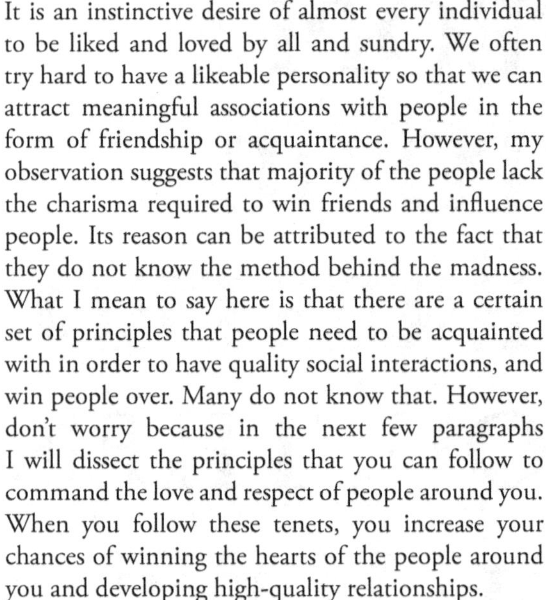

It is an instinctive desire of almost every individual to be liked and loved by all and sundry. We often try hard to have a likeable personality so that we can attract meaningful associations with people in the form of friendship or acquaintance. However, my observation suggests that majority of the people lack the charisma required to win friends and influence people. Its reason can be attributed to the fact that they do not know the method behind the madness. What I mean to say here is that there are a certain set of principles that people need to be acquainted with in order to have quality social interactions, and win people over. Many do not know that. However, don't worry because in the next few paragraphs I will dissect the principles that you can follow to command the love and respect of people around you. When you follow these tenets, you increase your chances of winning the hearts of the people around you and developing high-quality relationships.

In the past 100 years of modern self-help literature, there have been innumerable books written on the topics of personality development and self-improvement. Many of these books talk about how to get rich, boost self-confidence, conduct life and be the best version of yourself. The book that I am about to review in the following couple of pages can be considered a gold standard when it comes to self-help literature. It is "How to Win Friends and Influence People" by the maestro Dale Carnegie. This is a book that has been loved by millions of people around the globe because of its transformational nature. It has helped people shape up their personalities in a way that they become social magnets and start attracting

There are a certain set of principles that people need to be acquainted with in order to have quality social interactions and win people over.

This is a book that has been loved by millions of people around the globe because of its transformational nature. It has helped people shape up their personalities in a way that they become social magnets and start attracting quality people in their lives.

quality people in their lives. I have tried to extract the essence of this magnum opus by Carnegie in the following few paragraphs. So, let's get started.

This book will primarily help you achieve the following things:

- Improve your thought process and the way you conduct your daily life
- Develop your influence intrinsically
- Win over people by improving your inner/outer self
- Develop you as an engaging conversationalist
- Develop your network of associates and friends
- Create a powerful and conscientious personality

One of the first points Dale Carnegie stresses is the "Power of Listening." Most people tend to believe that being expressive and loud lubricates communication and makes it effective. However, that's not true. The first rule of seamless communication is that you have to be a very receptive listener. If you observe successful people around you, one thing that will stand out in their personality is the trait of active listening. They are zealously listening to people around them, picking up verbal and non-verbal cues and then responding accordingly. This helps them to be very firm, crisp, clear and concise when they talk. Whenever you interact or talk to someone, be genuinely interested in others. Don't focus on yourself during the conversation, give the other person a chance to speak. You can make these questions the staple of your communication. These will give you the ability to hear the other person out.

1. Ask them about their family and well being
2. What's going right or wrong for them
3. Is there anything you can help them with
4. Ask them about their future aspirations

Talk in a way that makes the other person realise that

If you observe successful people around you, one thing that will stand out in their personality is the trait of active listening. They are zealously listening to people around them, picking up verbal and non-verbal cues and then responding accordingly.

you are genuinely interested in them. This will enable you to develop healthy camaraderie with them which will enhance your influence.

The second critical point which can work wonders for you is learning to encourage and appreciate people. Very few people around you know the art of genuinely encouraging people and appreciating them for their achievements. Make sure not to confuse genuine praise with flattery. There is a principle in psychology known as Operant Conditioning according to which "a behaviour which is not rewarded will not be repeated." This means that if you fail to acknowledge people based on their good deeds the likelihood of repeating this event dilutes over time. Your honest praise of people will elevate your stature in the minds and hearts of people.

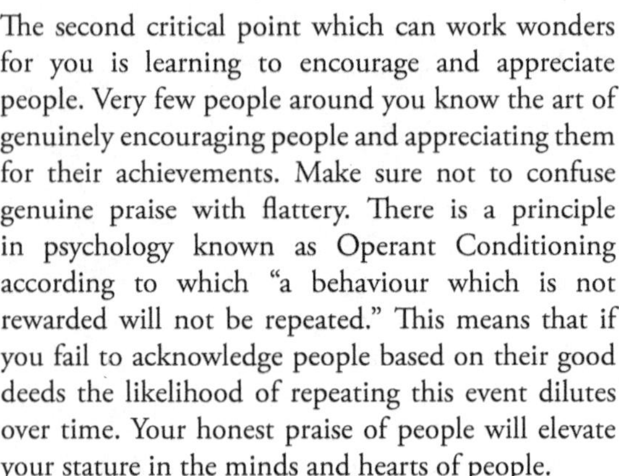

If you fail to acknowledge people based on their good deeds the likelihood of repeating this event dilutes over time. Your honest praise of people will elevate your stature in the minds and hearts of people.

There is a famous Chinese proverb that translates to "use your smile to change the world, don't let the world change your smile." Carnegie has specially focused on smile in this book and claims that such a trivial gesture can turn the tables for you. Smiling makes your personality likeable, acceptable and increases your chances of success. In the context of Pakistan, this is a dual edged sword. If a woman starts smiling at men, one can only imagine how the male community would respond. On the other hand, if a man starts passing a smile to women, then too the results can be guessed at. Therefore, you have to keep a balance when you smile and lace it with decency and sophistication.

Smiling makes your personality likeable, acceptable and increases your chances of success.

Keep a balance when you smile and lace it with decency and sophistication.

Almost all humans have a weakness of not admitting their mistakes. This is especially pervasive in our culture where every individual considers himself unassailable. On top of that, if you criticise or condemn them then it's totally unacceptable. Dale Carnegie understood this behaviour long time ago, so he added a point in this book which goes like this, "never criticise, condemn and complain about people." Whenever you criticise people, they get defensive and start repelling you. If you want to expand your network of associations and enhance your charisma then always explain things with love and compassion instead of picking on people.

Another very unique trick that you can use to influence people is to remember their names. Whenever you talk to them or have a conversation, always use their names while addressing them. The psychology behind this point is that whenever you call someone by his/her name Aisha, Saba, Kashif, Saleem, etc this is the sweetest sound for them in the entire world. You create good feelings, attraction and engagement which add value and weight to the conversation.

Another very unique trick that you can use to influence people is to remember their names. Whenever you talk to them or have a conversation, always use their names while addressing them.

I got to know about this book during my college days and promised myself that I will imbibe at least 50% of what this book teaches me. After all these years, I can safely say that I have retained at least 60% of this magnum opus by Carnegie. It has really helped me expand my influence and develop my personality. It can help you too, the onus is on you to get the ball rolling and take pragmatic actions to improve yourself.

PERSONAL NOTES

Use this space to write your notes and key takeaways from the book.

YOU WILL ONLY BE RELEVANT IF YOU ARE WILLING TO UNDO WHAT YOU HAVE LEARNT

THINK AGAIN

Author: Adam Grant
Genre: Self-help/Motivational

Mike Lazaridis was the man who, in the year 1999, made a path-breaking device that changed the way we live and work. The device was BlackBerry. It was so popular that it was used by leading CEOs of the world, top executives and even President of the USA. They had fallen in love with the first smartphone the world had ever seen. Back in the year 2009, BlackBerry owned 50% of the US smartphone market and enjoyed the status of being an incumbent. Lo and behold, in the next five years its market share had fallen from 50% to 1%. A colossal company faced bankruptcy within just a matter of a few years. Many reasons can be attributed to the sharp decline of BlackBerry but the most pivotal and potent reason is failure to "Think Again."

Many reasons can be attributed to the sharp decline of BlackBerry but the most pivotal and potent reason is failure to "Think Again."

Mike Lazaridis was a genius from childhood, a wonder kid. During the course of his life, he performed several remarkable feats, the best one of them is the invention of BlackBerry. However, despite being so sharp, intelligent and clever he had a major flaw in his personality that eventually led to the decline of his company. This was his inability to unlearn and relearn. Technology was moving at the speed of light around him but he was oblivious to this change. Steve Jobs, in the year 2007, launched the iPhone which overwhelmed people with a keyboard-less touchscreen, hence revolutionising the entire smartphone landscape. Lazaridis was adamant that people only needed a mobile with a keyboard and the rest is history.

This example is the essence of this remarkable

book by Adam Grant titled "Think Again." It is an absolute masterpiece that provides a scintillating and riveting account of the perils of stagnancy of thought and the benefits of rewiring and retooling to become future-proof. This book lets you dig deep inside yourself and shakes you to the core. It provides the impetus and inspiration to always keep moving and progressing to stay relevant.

It is an absolute masterpiece that provides a scintillating and riveting account of the perils of stagnancy of thought and the benefits of rewiring and retooling to become future-proof.

Adam Grant explains that there are typically four types of people. First come prosecutors who are present in large numbers in a society. Their job is to complain and find fault in everything. They belong to the category of "Know it all" people who consider themselves as the authority in every field of life. Since they already know everything, therefore, they don't consider it wise enough to exert themselves to learn anything new hence becoming stagnant after a period of time. The second category of people are the preachers. These people are great advisers but leave the logic behind in matters of life. Therefore, change never happens. The third category is politicians. They are power-hungry and to reach a certain level of success they use treachery and deceit instead of knowledge, wisdom and skill. The final category is that of the scientists. They throw superstitious ideologies and pre-established societal norms out of the window. For them, there is only one guiding force in their lives and that is logic. This category of people put their belief in experimentation, observation and research due to which they are in a continuous process of improvement. Eventually, the world follows them owing to their intellect and progressive approach towards life. Allama Iqbal, the great poet proclaims their uniqueness in following couplet.

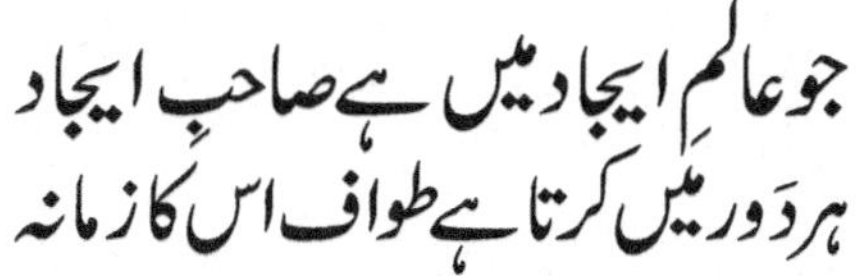

Being a scientist doesn't mean that you are a quintessential scientist who knows about physics, chemistry or biology. Adam Grant uses this umbrella term for those people who continuously stay in learning mode and who refuse to let their ideas become their ideologies. These people use research, curiosity, skepticism and doubt to provide them with an anchor in life.

It was this curiosity that made a clerk in a Swiss patent office, Albert Einstein, such an accomplished individual. Therefore, don't be driven by dogmas and ideologies in your life. Even the Holy Quran reiterates the importance of reflection, observation and experimentation.

- And of His signs is the creation of heavens and earth, and the diversity of your tongues and colours. No doubt, in it are signs for those who hear (30:22)
- And he has made to work for you whatsoever is in the heavens and whatsoever is in the earth by His Command. Verily in it are signs for the people who reflect (45:13)

It is clear from these verses that Allah says think, research, ponder and observe. People who can do it eventually become the likes of of Alexander Fleming, Albert Einstein and Stephen Hawking.

Another amazing and interesting concept that Adam Grant discusses in this book is pertaining to the Dunning-Kruger Effect. David Dunning and Justin Kruger published a famous report a few years back in which their finding was that incompetent people tend to have higher confidence. They performed a series of studies that reflected that people with the lowest score in logical reasoning, grammar and sense of humor had a high opinion about their abilities.

These are the set of people who while sitting at home

give expert advise to the likes of Babar Azam and Virat Kohli on the art of batting. They are called "armchair quarterbacks", it's a condition in which confidence exceeds competence. Never be trapped in such a psychological quagmire. Your competence needs to go hand in hand with your confidence. You should always be inquisitive to know more and focus on things that you don't know about.

Adam Grant also lays stress on collective rethinking. He says that educational institutions, especially teachers, should promote lifelong learning instead of being fixated on lectures and slide shows. Teachers need to cultivate curiosity, disseminate doubt and encourage the courage to question. Only by doing this can the world produce individuals who are thoughtful and progressive. The ultimate goal of this book is to instill in an individual the humility, capacity and willingness to question his ideologies, rewire his beliefs and retool himself to stay relevant.

Adam Grant also lays stress on collective rethinking. He says that educational institutions, especially teachers, should promote lifelong learning instead of being fixated on lectures and slide shows.

PERSONAL NOTES

Use this space to write your notes and key takeaways from the book.

THE DARK SIDE OF LAHORE

TABOO

Author: Dr. Fouzia Saeed
Genre: Sociology

Lahore is considered to be the cultural capital of Pakistan. There is a famous saying in Punjabi about the city which goes like this *"Jinay Lor Ni Wekheya O Jameya Nae"* which means an individual who hasn't seen Lahore hasn't been born. It is indeed a beautiful city with a remarkable history. Modern Lahore can rival any city in the world due to its modern infrastructure, roads, cleanliness and transport network. However, there are a few areas in Lahore which are notorious for the activities that are performed there. All of us have seen Minar-e-Pakistan, Badshahi mosque and Shahi Qila but there is an area right next to these historical places which is famous for its immoral activities known as Heera Mandi or Bazaar-e-Husn. It won't be wrong to call this area as the hub of prostitution in Pakistan.

Dr. Fouzia Saeed, in the year 2001, wrote a remarkable book titled "Taboo" which explored the dark world of Heera Mandi. She collated first-hand information that she got during her ethnographic research and compiled it in the form of a book. This book is a comprehensive crash course to understand the institution of prostitution in South Asia. This is the reason why it has been translated into several languages, making it one of the best pieces of literature in this category.

Dr. Fouzia writes that since she was a government servant at the time of her research for this book, she had to face a lot of hurdles and red tape from the bureaucracy. It seemed as if some people in power wanted to cover up the stories of this neighborhood due to the fact that there are many secrets of the rich

and powerful buried in the old and shabby homes of the prostitutes. She extrapolates her research in the form of a storyline that is very riveting and interesting. Several characters like Mehmood Kanjar, Chanda, Laila, Pammi, Nargis, Faiza lace up the story and reveal the never before known secrets of this dark world. Let's get to know what they are.

The people living in Heera Mandi are known by their profession which means that their work determines their caste. Let's first talk about the musicians who are known as "Mirasi." Mirasi is a word derived from a word known as Miras which means "lineage."

Back in the day, these people used to dance and provide entertainment at the weddings of landlords and rich people. Mirasi's are professional musicians and play the instruments behind the dancing girls. All of the people in this profession are males since it is almost impossible for a woman to earn a livelihood by playing music.

Next comes "Tawaif", whose main profession is dancing. From the time of Mughals, or even before them, these women have been enchanting their customers through their dance performances. "Kotha" is the place where she lives and presents her mujra (dance performance). The aim of Tawaif is to entertain her customers as much as possible through her sensual dance performance so she can reap maximum money out of them. These women are so refined and cultured in their talk and demeanor that back in the day rich people used to send their children to them so that they can learn manners and etiquettes.

The aim of Tawaif is to entertain her customers as much as possible through her sensual dance performance so she can reap maximum money out of them.

Let's talk about the "Kanjar" community now who are directly involved in the business of prostitution. Kanjar is an ethnic group or caste who since centuries have been involved in providing sexual pleasure to their customers. A female prostitute is known as a

Kanjar is an ethnic group or caste who since centuries have been involved in providing sexual pleasure to their customers.

"Kanjari." In Pakistani culture, deep inside it is the desire of every woman to have a son. Celebrations are held on the birth of a son and everyone is happy since he is the ultimate heir to the family. However, in the Kanjar community, the opposite happens; celebrations happen when a girl is born while the birth of the boy is looked down upon. This is because a woman is the head of the family in this community and it is her job to run the finances of the house. As long as she trades her body in exchange for money things will be on track. The more girls there are in the family, the better it is for them.

The most painful ritual performed by these people is that of "Nath Utarvai." As soon as a girl reaches the age of puberty, her mother or her Naika start their hunt to find her first customer. Naika is considered to be a manager in this profession who manages all the financial matters of the prostitute. Nath Utarvai is a dreadful ritual that is related to the girl losing her virginity. Naika tries to raise the best offer so a large sum of money can be obtained. If they can find a good customer and the bid is high, the whole family celebrates and everyone is informed about the deal. Nath Utarwai signals the start of the career for the prostitute who then bears fatherless children and lives the most dreadful life. Their minds since childhood are so meticulously tuned that they slip very naturally into this profession without any raving and ranting.

The most painful ritual performed by these people is that of "Nath Utarvai." As soon as a girl reaches the age of puberty, her mother or her Naika start their hunt to find her first customer.

Another important character of this network is the "Dalal" also known as the pimp. This is the individual who is at the lowest level of this social hierarchy. His job is to find clients for the prostitutes and crack the deal. Whatever prostitutes earn, a small portion of that money is given to him as well.

The women working as prostitutes in Heera Mandi can be segregated into three categories. The girls belonging to the "A" category are literate, can speak

English well, and are beautiful. These girls have a limited set of rich customers. Some of the girls from this category go on to venture into TV dramas and films as well. Next is the "B" category, these are the girls who run the quintessential brothel in the Mandi. They face maximum oppression from the government and police since they do their business very openly. Last is the "C" category. These are the ones who are usually older in age and were not able to maintain their brothel due to financial crunch. Women living on Tibbi street in the Heera Mandi fall into this category. They trade their body for only Rs. 500 or Rs.1000.

Most people consider poverty to be the root cause of this evil. However, despite being an Islamic country, what is the reason that such areas still exist? Dr. Fouzia writes that instead of poverty it is the supervision of the rich and powerful that has kept these areas alive. People in power over the course of centuries have been developing, institutionalising, and protecting these prostitutes.

Dr. Fouzia writes that instead of poverty it is the supervision of the rich and powerful that has kept these areas alive. People in power over the course of centuries have been developing, institutionalising, and protecting these prostitutes.

Around 2300 years ago at the time of Chandragupta Maurya, there was a comprehensive system of managing prostitution. The government protected the institution of prostitution and collected taxes. These women were also used as intelligence agents. The government used to appoint a superintendent to manage this profession. It was his job to ensure that the girls are taught dance and music so the ruling elite can be entertained. At the time of Akbar when prostitution began to get out of control, he appointed a secretary whose job was to keep it under check. He consolidated a community of about 6,000 houses and turned it into a mass brothel called Shaitanpura. The British continued this tradition and further supported these women. In fact, Anarkali was the place in Lahore where the British settled prostitutes.

Around 2300 years ago at the time of Chandragupta Maurya, there was a comprehensive system of managing prostitution. The government protected the institution of prostitution and collected taxes. These women were also used as intelligence agents.

Dr. Fouzia Saeed believes that the source of this evil

lies in our patriarchal society where male domination leads to abominations towards women. Some people might agree with it while some might not. The truth is that prostitution is considered to be the oldest profession in the world and somewhere poverty and financial dependence are big factors for its pervasiveness across all societies.

My recommendation is that before more areas like Heera Mandi become pervasive in our country, it is the responsibility of the government to ensure that every person should get all the required financial and economic opportunities to maintain their social stature and live a good life. In addition, as a responsible citizen of Pakistan, it is indispensable for us to contribute towards the upliftment of our society in every way, especially financially and economically so no more Lailas, Chandas and Pammis have to see a brothel ever again.

Dr. Fouzia Saeed believes that the source of this evil lies in our patriarchal society where male domination leads to abomination towards women.

PERSONAL NOTES

Use this space to write your notes and key takeaways from the book.

PERSONAL NOTES

Use this space to write your notes and key takeaways from the book.

WE BECOME WHAT WE THINK ABOUT

THE SECRET
Author: Rhonda Byrne
Genre: Self-help/Motivational

Twelve years ago, I saw a video on YouTube that transformed my thought process and in turn my life. The message in the video was so powerful that I still remember the essence of it very clearly. Whenever I face ambiguity in life, I go back to the same video to seek inspiration. I will let you in on its name at the end of this review but for now, we will focus on a book that carries a similar message. This book has taken the world of self-help by storm and has broken all sales records. Its simple yet profound message is so easy to understand that it can result in a complete transformation of your life. The name of the book is "The Secret" by Rhonda Byrne. It was published in the year 2006 and since that time onwards it has become a global best seller.

The book alludes to a famous concept in the world of self-help literature which pertains to the "Law of Attraction." In a nutshell, this means, "thoughts become reality." Whatever your mind can conceive it can achieve if you have the conviction, determination, and perseverance to pursue your dreams. If you want a big house, a good car, a good job or a foreign tour just think about it with conviction and eventually, you will start attracting all these things in your life. Similarly, if you are a pessimist and negative thinker you will attract the same negativity in your life. In the language of The Secret, this is known as "thoughts behind things." Rhonda Byrne says that each person is like a transmission tower with different frequencies. Whenever this frequency collides with another common frequency in the universe things start happening. For example, if you aspire to own a Honda Civic and that frequency blends in with the

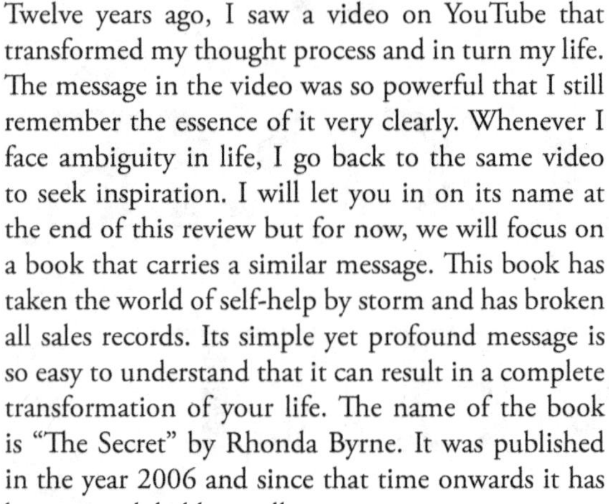

frequency of the car then a time will come when you will own a Honda Civic in reality.

This comes across as a metaphysical concept, which it actually is. However, this is what the self-help genre is all about. You take up any great motivational book whether it be Rich Dad Poor Dad, Think and Grow Rich or The Magic of Thinking Big, the common focal point of all these books is the law of attraction.

These sorts of concepts take the readers to a crossroads sometimes. There is a large section of society, especially in our part of the world, who have blind faith in destiny. People live their entire lives as slaves of their fate *(Kismet)*. They believe in a deterministic approach where all good and bad things happen in life because they are predestined. The Secret turns this entire concept on its head by promulgating the concept of man being the master of his destiny. It promotes the concept of free will which illustrates the fact that a man can change the course of his life with his hard work and conviction. It solidifies the beliefs in one's own strength and pushes an individual to achieve anything in life.

There is a large section of society especially in our part of the world who have blind faith in destiny. People live their entire lives as slaves of their fate (kismet). They believe in a deterministic approach where all good and bad things happen in life because they are already written.

If you look around and observe people, you will very soon conclude that those who believe in free will and have a passion to achieve excellence are most likely to be more successful and happier than the ones who believe in fate as the only reality of life. The Secret advocates the same as well. Now the question comes whether all these are arbitrary discussions or is there an objective way of attracting positive things in our lives. The good news is that there is surely a way and it's very easy to execute as well.

If you look around and observe people, you will very soon conclude that those who believe in free will and have a passion to achieve excellence are most likely to be more successful and happier than the ones who believe in fate as the only reality of life.

You will need three things to get started; a diary, a pen and your thoughts. The first step is to write all the things that you want in your life- a high-paying job, a Mercedes car, a big home, a beautiful wife, etc. The second step might sound delusionary but it actually works really well. What you need to do is to think that you have already got these things in your life. The third step is visualisation, which means that you have to make a picture in your mind which shows how will you feel when you achieve all this.

There is nothing in the world that you cannot achieve if you start thinking consistently and compassionately about your desires. This is the sole message in this book.

Now back to that video I talked about at the start of this review. If you are curious, go to YouTube and type "The Strangest Secret by Earl Nightingale." A 35 minute video will appear in front of you. Click the video, since it might just change your life. However, do that once you finish Readistan.

There is nothing in the world that you cannot achieve if you start thinking consistently and compassionately about your desires.

PERSONAL NOTES

Use this space to write your notes and key takeaways from the book.

PERSONAL NOTES

Use this space to write your notes and key takeaways from the book.

DREAMS ARE A MANIFESTATION OF OUR REPRESSED DESIRES

THE INTERPRETATION OF DREAMS

Author: Sigmund Freud
Genre: Psychology

Every one of you who is reading this text must have witnessed dreams during sleep. Sometimes dreams are magical and bizarre while other times they are scary and obscure. Have you ever tried to explore what is the essence of the dream that you saw last night? We are often confused about the connection of the content of our dreams with our real lives. Some people are so obsessed with their dreams that they go to great lengths to get them decoded, sometimes seeking the help of a saint or a psychologist.

The world of dreams is often outlandish, eccentric, freakish and illogical. Superficially, it doesn't seem to have any solid connection with the real world. Many stalwarts of psychology and men of science have tried to explain dreams and their implications in our daily life. However, none has been more influential and controversial than the king of psychoanalysis, Sigmund Freud. Freud is a colossal figure in the field of psychology, specially psychoanalysis, who through his path-breaking concepts progressed the science of psychology and in turn, created a very polarised community of psychologists who tend to have mixed views about his contribution to the discipline. Many regard him as a genius (which he actually was) while others write him off by labelling his concepts as frivolous and untrue.

The world of dreams is often outlandish, eccentric, freakish, and illogical. Superficially, it doesn't seem to have any solid connection with the real world.

In the year 1900, Sigmund Freud published his seminal work on the subject of dreams titled "Die Traumdeutung" translated as The Interpretation of Dreams. This book can be considered his magnum opus since it gives insights into important concepts of human psychology like dreams, the unconscious

and the Oedipus Complex. The Interpretation of Dreams catapulted Freud to stardom despite the fact that it took ten long years to sell out the first edition (which had only 600 copies). As time went by, its popularity started snowballing and eventually made it one of the most sought-after pieces of literature in the world of psychology.

The Interpretation of Dreams catapulted Freud to stardom despite the fact that it took ten long years to sell out the first edition.

This book is basically an analysis of the dreams of his patients. Sigmund Freud was a psychoanalyst and he used to treat people using lengthy psychoanalytical processes. Prior to publishing The Interpretation of Dreams, Freud had analysed over 1000 dreams of his patients and collated his findings in the form of this book. Here are some of the peculiar takeaways of his analysis.

Prior to publishing The Interpretation of Dreams, Freud had analysed over 1000 dreams of his patients and collated his findings in the form of this book.

Freud advocated the idea that dreams are comprised of latent content and manifest content. The manifest content is the actual storyline that is played during the dream. It is what we see through the eye of our brain when we are dreaming. For instance, many people fall off a tall building during sleep, a few people meet their lovers, while a few travel on a train during sleep. The latent content on the other hand is the hidden underlying and covert meaning of the dream.

Freud wrote that most dreams are caused by memories of our past. Dreams specially use our childhood memories and manifest them in various shapes and forms during our dreams. Another key finding of his research was that the dreams are offshoots of our repressed wishes and desires which have not been fulfilled. There are innumerable amount of wishes and aspirations that remain unfulfilled during the course of life of every individual. These repressed wishes make their way to the unconscious mind where they become transmission engines for the content of our dreams. Through dreams, we try to fulfill those unfulfilled wishes to maintain the

Another key finding of his research was that the dreams are offshoots of our repressed wishes and desires which have not been fulfilled.

equilibrium of our personality. Dreams provide us a window of opportunity through which we can gain what we have lost in the real world.

One of the most controversial finding of this book is that the fundamental basis of our dreams are the restrained sexual desires that we are not able to put to action in real life. These sexual desires eventually find their expression through dreams. He further goes on to discuss a bizarre concept in the book known as "Oedipus Complex." He claims it to be a phase in the life of a child whereby he experiences sexual attraction towards parent of the opposite sex. For example, a girl will be sexually attracted to her father and a boy to his mother.

One of the key takeaways of the book is Freud's explanation of the "unconscious mind" which he believes controls our dreams and the major part of our daily life. Our brain is like an iceberg where 10%-20% is the conscious mind while the invisible 80% is the unconscious mind. While dreaming our unconscious mind transforms our repressed desires into illogical and meaningless objects which we often tend to see. This is deliberately done so the conscious mind cannot detect our true feelings and we can escape the embarrassment. You can understand these phenomena from the following thought experiment.

You have an aspiration to marry the most beautiful woman in the world, she can be an actress, a princess or your neighbour; but she is out of your reach. In your dream, you will not be marrying her directly rather it will be the other way around. In your dream, you might be her servant, her courtier, her driver or her doctor. This happens because your unconscious mind tries to fool your conscious mind into believing that you are not interested in the lady at all. As soon as you wake up, your conscious mind is back in control while your unconscious mind suppresses its thoughts and desires right there. This is the reason

why you often fail to recall your dreams because your mind deliberately forgets the embarrassment that the dream might cause you.

Freud had to face a lot of aggressive opposition due to his outrageous ideas. Some of his students eventually went on to oppose his theories and tried to prove him wrong. Most psychologists reject Freud's psychoanalysis as unscientific and redundant.

Whatever the case may be, Freud is one of the most influential figures in the field of psychology. He was a scholar who dared to explore new avenues of human psychology and was not afraid to voice his opinion. You might agree or disagree with his point of view however, you can never disregard his contributions in understanding the deep, complex and dynamic idiosyncrasies of human psychology.

Freud had to face a lot of aggressive opposition due to his outrageous ideas. Some of his students eventually went on to oppose his theories and tried to prove him wrong.

PERSONAL NOTES

Use this space to write your notes and key takeaways from the book.

BEGIN WITH THE END IN MIND

THE 7 HABITS OF HIGHLY EFFECTIVE PEOPLE
Author: Stephen Covey
Genre: Self-help

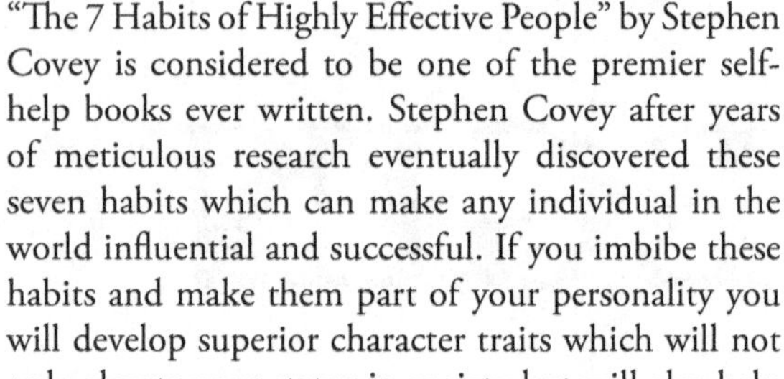

"The 7 Habits of Highly Effective People" by Stephen Covey is considered to be one of the premier self-help books ever written. Stephen Covey after years of meticulous research eventually discovered these seven habits which can make any individual in the world influential and successful. If you imbibe these habits and make them part of your personality you will develop superior character traits which will not only elevate your status in society but will also help you achieve great feats in life. Let's decode what these seven habits are.

According to Stephen Covey, the first habit of influential people is their proactive nature. They do not surrender themselves to the hands of fate rather, they are the creators of their own destiny. They have a strong belief in the fact that whatever happens in their life, it is a direct consequence of their decisions. They refuse to comply with the superficial standards set by society and tread their own path. In contrast, reactive people can always be observed complaining and blaming their circumstances. You will often hear them using these phrases "I am not lucky", "I am not successful because my boss is toxic", "I could not progress in life because my family was poor", "I had to make a lot of compromises in life because of my family and society which makes me unhappy." All these are signs of a fixed and failed mindset.

The second habit of highly effective people is that they always begin with the end in mind. Ultimately everyone has to leave the world and we need to keep asking ourselves the question that when we die what do we want people to say at our funeral. Almost all of us would want people to remember us as a good husband, a good son, a good painter, a good businessman, a brilliant orator or a good artist etc. If we want people to write a good epitaph for us then we need to start working on all these qualities from today. These qualities that you want to imbibe in your personality will become your guiding force. For instance, I have an aspiration that when I die, I would want people to remember me as a reformist who influenced millions of lives through his intellect and wisdom. If I intend for people to remember me as a man of vision and execution, then it is my greatest obligation in life to work towards it.

The third habit of highly effective people is to "put first things first." Successful people always know how to prioritise things and never look for excuses to shun responsibility. I often find people complaining about lack of time to kick off any of their personal initiatives but in my opinion, an individual can achieve anything in a span of 24 hours provided he has the motivation and drive to do so. Unsuccessful people just keep scrolling through their mobile phones, making timetables or making lengthy plans instead of being pragmatic and biased towards action. If you learn to prioritise things in your life then there is nothing in this world that you can't achieve. If you are a laggard and an expert procrastinator then time will never be on your side and you will perennially chase things.

The third habit of highly effective people is to "put first things first." Successful people always know how to prioritise things and never look for excuses to shun responsibility.

There is a phrase in the English language that goes like this: "my way or the highway." Stephen Covey really abhorred this approach and didn't agree with it at all. He always believed that being successful should not come at the cost of the failure of others, rather it should always be a win-win situation for both parties involved. Influential people are always empathetic towards others and respect the perspective and ideology of their counterparts. This

Influential people always succeed by lifting others and making them successful.

leads us to the fourth habit and that is to "create a win-win situation." Influential people always succeed by lifting others and making them successful.

The fifth habit of effective people is that they are always interested in understanding others instead of being self-centric and narcissistic i.e. they seek to understand rather than to be understood. Such people are amazing listeners and always act with empathy. This habit helps them create deeper and more profound bonds with people around them since they understand their feelings, give them value and respect their dignity. Strong listening skills help them develop a greater understanding of human nature due to which they respond most appropriately to people from all walks of life.

The fifth habit of effective people is that they are always interested in understanding others instead of being self-centric and narcissistic i.e., they seek to understand rather than to be understood.

The sixth habit pertains to synergy. These people always cherish working in teams towards the attainment of a specific purpose since they believe that progress lies in collective wisdom. I have personally observed that the more you work with people and refrain from taking a solo flight, the more chances you have of success, growth and progress. Creating synergy leads to the achievement of bigger feats in life that cannot be surmounted alone.

The sixth habit pertains to synergy. These people always cherish working in teams towards the attainment of a specific purpose since they believe that progress lies in collective wisdom.

The seventh habit is to "sharpen the saw." This refers to the fact that you have to spend your whole life developing your abilities, capabilities, skills and competencies. The more you polish your skills, the more you will grow in life. Therefore, if you aspire to reach a state of self-actualization in life then always be on the move and keep sharpening your saw. If you want to get fit then ensure that you work out regularly, if you want to have a sharp and creative mind then put it to use through regular reading and learning, if you are always short of time then enroll in a time management course and learn to manage your clock. Remember: Action cures fear.

In the modern dynamic world, where things are becoming obsolete at the speed of light, merely sticking to a single skill thinking that it will last a lifetime is not a sensible decision. In the knowledge economy of today, loaded with big data, virtual reality and robots you need to keep yourself abreast with all the latest trends so that you stay relevant in the game.

These seven habits are truly remarkable and have helped millions of people around the globe to transform their lives for good. I would like to add an eighth habit (Stephen Covey has already written a book with the same title) to the already existing seven and that is "Perseverance." When all things fail in life, the ability to persevere takes an individual through. I have seen many people with average intellect and talent being outrageously successful due to their perseverance and commitment to a cause. Sticking to a long-term goal with utmost steadfastness can help you achieve great things in life.

PERSONAL NOTES

Use this space to write your notes and key takeaways from the book.

FRIENDSHIP IN A MARITAL RELATIONSHIP LEADS TO ITS SUCCESS

THE SEVEN PRINCIPLES FOR MAKING MARRIAGE WORK

Author: John Gottman
Genre: Psychology

In the year 1986, John Gottman, who was a professor of psychology at the University of Washington, established a research lab by the name of "Love Lab." The sole purpose of establishing this lab was to scientifically find out the reasons that can make a marriage work. This was the first research ever on this topic which spanned across 14 years. As part of it, around 650 couples were meticulously studied. On the basis of the findings of this research, Gottman published a path-breaking book in the year 1999 titled "The Seven Principles for Making Marriage Work." You might have read a few books on relationship management but this book by John Gottman stands out due to its evidence-based and data-backed propositions. If you or anyone around you is going through a tough time in their marriage, then read the next few paragraphs with full attention-they might provide you the solution that you need.

This book busts a few myths that society has established when it comes to marital relationship. For instance, we tend to believe that the couples who are the happiest never get into any brawl or argument. A flawless husband-wife relationship is sans any fight. However, the book suggests that the happiest couples do get into arguments, conflicts and verbal fights but they are experts in conflict management. They may quarrel or have a strong difference of opinion in various matters of life but they overcome those conflicts resulting in the resumption of an amicable and loving relationship. Therefore, if you are having daily bouts of altercations with your spouse then learn the art of managing it. This will help in the longevity of your partnership.

Now, when it comes to conflict management, I have often heard marriage counsellors rating communication between couples as the most vital organ of a fulfilling relationship. They always advocate cliched virtues of empathy, compromise, listening to your partner and adaptability. Gottman rubbishes this argument and says that when one partner is in a listening mode then usually the counterpart is in a bashing mode who vents out all their anger and disagreements. This in turn incites the other person to respond back and eventually things get heated. Instead, Gottman, through research, found out that 69% of the conflicts in a marriage cannot be resolved. They are perpetual and irresoluble which means that come what may, they will continue to linger on. For instance, when a Punjabi boy marries a Pakhtun girl and their child is born, there is a disagreement between the couple as to which language their child will speak. Another source of conflict might be the husband's flirtatious nature at parties or any family gathering. Similarly, couples might get into arguments on the number of children they would like to have. Usually, these sorts of issues do not have straightforward solutions since neither party is willing to give in. Therefore, smart and happy couples firstly acknowledge this disconnect, respect each other's opinions and move on with their lives without getting into any further arguments.

Another peculiar thing that Gottman highlights is that after years of research on married couples, he could predict with 91% accuracy whether in the future this couple will opt for a divorce or not. He mentions a few factors which can be used to predict the possibility of a divorce. They are:

1. Harsh Startups – it means always starting the conversation on a negative note through a taunt, complaint, or criticism
2. Emotional Flooding – it means bashing your partner so much on an everyday basis that he/she gets drained emotionally and loses interest

or engagement in the relationship

Now let's move towards the million-dollar question, what makes a marriage work? The single biggest reason behind happily married couples is friendship. When friendship prevails between husband and wife, it enables them to enjoy their association due to mutual admiration and respect. This makes arguments, conflict and disagreements take a back seat. Gottman proclaims that the essence of the marriage is to have common aims, goals and objectives where partners engage actively in helping each other. A marriage gets off-track when continuously one partner has to sacrifice their dreams and compromise on every matter of life. This breeds bitterness and dilutes the status of a healthy partnership. Usually, in our part of the world, it is the woman who has to compromise most of the time.

Speaking of friendship, the next step is to see what it takes to cultivate friendship in a couple. There are three rules to follow in this regard.

1. Take interest in your partner's interest – this is a key point in developing healthy camaraderie with your spouse.
2. Appreciation – learn to appreciate and support each other in the most trivial of things.
3. Influence – learn to respect the decisions of your partner.

Marriage is one of the most important decisions that an individual takes in his life. If you find a good partner, it can indeed be one of the greatest blessings. The institution of marriage of late has been under great threat in the West and the same threat is now making its way to our part of the world. Generation Z is somehow reluctant to get married due to the pressure of obligation or commitment. In these testing times, people like John Gottman and their literature can really improve people's lives. What do you think?

The single biggest reason behind happily married couples is friendship. When friendship prevails between husband and wife it enables them to enjoy their association due to mutual admiration and respect.

A marriage gets off-track when continuously one partner has to sacrifice their dreams and compromise on every matter of life.

IF GIVEN A
CHOICE, IT
IS BETTER
FOR A
PRINCE TO
BE FEARED
RATHER
THAN BEING
LOVED

THE PRINCE
Author: Niccolo Machiavelli
Genre: Philosophy

Should a prince be feared or should he be loved by his people? How should a king or a ruler of a country behave? Moreover, what does a prince need to do to stay in power and increase the longevity of his rule? What sort of behavioral patterns do corporate leaders and politicians need to possess so that the people around them stay loyal and faithful to them? In the next few paragraphs, you will get the answer to all these questions as I dissect an absolute cult classic book titled "The Prince" by Niccolo Machiavelli.

The Prince is considered to be a bible of political philosophy which is a narrative on how a leader should behave. Over the years, it has exercised great influence in the political and corporate fraternity due to its controversial and cutthroat philosophy. The central theme of the book is to keep the prince or the rulers of any kingdom intact, even if it has to be done through immoral means. It is a must-read for individuals who aspire to be leaders or who are already in a leadership position. It is a complete treatise on how a leader should conduct his life whether it be through treachery or cunningness.

Niccolo Machiavelli was an Italian philosopher and diplomat who gained global fame due to his magnum opus, The Prince. In this book, he writes about the prince of his time Lorenzo de' Medici and provides him with a set of instructions that he needs to follow in order to strengthen his grip on his people and subsequently his territory. Let's discuss the most important takeaways from this masterpiece.

Let's allude to the question with which I started

this review. Should a prince be feared or should he be loved by his people? Machiavelli advocates the fact that a king should both be loved and feared. However, he believes that in reality, it's not possible that someone can be loved and feared at the same time. Therefore, if given an option a leader or a prince should decide to be feared rather than being loved. It's safer to be feared than to be loved. He claims that when a prince is bonded with his people via love, this leads to an obligation-based relationship and when people are bound by obligation, they become fickle. The bond of love is weak and is only in place as long as you are in a position of strength and power. On the other hand, relationship of fear is preserved by punishment. Whenever people are afraid of punishment, they will always be faithful to you. A prince should create an image where people fear him and in turn, stay loyal to him.

If given an option a leader or a prince should decide to be feared rather than being loved. It's safer to be feared than to be loved.

Machiavelli presents a stunning recommendation on the art of dealing with flatterers. He writes that it is impossible for a prince to escape flattery therefore it is better to have a strategy of handling it. He proposes that the prince should encourage honesty and bluntness amongst his people so that they do not get into a habit of apple polishing. However, there is a flip side to this: if everyone comes and speaks his heart out in front of the prince, he will gradually start losing his prestige and value. Over the course of time, his fear in the hearts of people will start diluting which can have an adverse effect on his kingdom. In order to avoid this scenario, Machiavelli proposes an interesting solution. A prince needs to select two to three people from his team who are his confidants. Only these people should be allowed to confront the prince, talk back to him and be viciously honest. The prince should act in a way whereby whoever is the most transparent with him should be rewarded the most. This will help him stay grounded and keep a check on reality.

A prince needs to select two to three people from his team who are his confidants. Only these people should be allowed to confront the prince, talk back to him and be viciously honest.

Another important postulate of Machiavelli is that the prince should be very well trained in the art of war. This is even more relevant and important in times of peace so that he doesn't get complacent and learns the tips and tricks required to win a war. We can draw meaning from these instructions to suit modern times as well. In the corporate world, when leaders make their company successful and numero uno, they tend to relax, become complacent and enjoy the feeling of being the incumbent. A classical case in point is that of BlackBerry, Kodak and Blockbuster. These companies were at the top of their game but due to the inability of their leaders to foresee the future, they are history today. Therefore, it is absolutely indispensable for leaders to keep an eye on the dynamic environment around them so they know when to change and adapt. This helps them keep the competition at bay and prepare for tough times.

Another important aspect that this book alludes to is the selection of a secretary for the prince. A prince is known by the people he is surrounded by so if his associates are smart and intelligent it will give a positive perception about the prince and vice versa. Therefore, it is important to have an intelligent secretary in place. A litmus test to witness the effectiveness of a secretary is that he should always keep the interest of the prince above his personal interests. His life and death should be to serve the prince and nothing else. He should extend unconditional support to the prince and keep all his personal gains secondary. Machiavelli acknowledges the fact that it is hard to find these sorts of people. However, once you do find them hold them tight and reward them generously.

Another very critical point highlighted by the great author in this book is about taking sides during a battle or a war. He categorically states that the prince should either be a friend or an enemy with

It is absolutely indispensable for leaders to keep an eye on the dynamic environment around them so they know when to change and adapt.

A litmus test to witness the effectiveness of a secretary is that he should always keep the interest of the prince above his personal interests. His life and death should be to serve the prince and nothing else.

The prince should either be a friend or an enemy with his counterpart rulers. There should be nothing in between, no grey area. There is no concept of being neutral in the wisdom of Machiavelli.

his counterpart rulers. There should be nothing in between, no grey area. There is no concept of being neutral in the wisdom of Machiavelli. He builds a strong case to support his argument. According to Machiavelli, being decisive works under all conditions. For instance, if the prince wins the war along with his associates they are bound by obligation. Even if the winner is any of his counterparts, they will respect him since the prince had extended support to them during the war. In case of loss, he will still be better off since he will have accomplices who will continue to be on his side. This will keep him safe under all conditions.

Many commentators while reviewing the prince consider it as a work of deceit and treachery. I have a very clear perspective on this. Hypocrisy, trickery, chicanery and deception are part of human nature therefore, you can't sweep them under the carpet. These traits along with other positive attributes construct the personality of an individual. I feel it is really important to study the dark side of human nature as well and how people make use of it to further their own interests. Reading the prince doesn't bind you to follow whatever has been written rather, a well-formed and well-nurtured mind is always aware of the narrative and counter-narrative. It then formulates its own understanding and opinions based on its personal understanding of life. Therefore, I urge you to read and understand what according to you is counter-intuitive and not in resonance with your thought process. This will help you develop a mature mind which in turn will enable you to make high-quality decisions in life.

PERSONAL NOTES

Use this space to write your notes and key takeaways from the book.

TO BE HAPPY, ONE MUST FIRST NOT BE UNHAPPY

THE CONQUEST OF HAPPINESS
Author: Bertrand Russell
Genre: Philosophy

It is the desire of almost every individual to be happy in life except for the people who are suffering from anhedonia. Almost all of us try our level best to do all those things which contribute towards our happiness. However, if you look at the happiness index of 8 Billion people in the world, you will infer that most of us spend our lives in great sorrow and unhappiness. This unhappiness can be attributed to many reasons like lack of resources, failure to attain the desired social status, not possessing a good car or a house, dearth of quality friends or associations in life and the list is never-ending.

Over the years people have laid great emphasis on finding out the reasons behind the unhappiness of people. However, almost ninety years ago Bertrand Russell, a maestro, a guru and a legendary author wrote a breathtaking book in which he summarised the root causes behind happiness and unhappiness in life. It's titled "The Conquest of Happiness." Russell is such an articulate individual that when he writes it feels as if your emotions are dancing in front of you on the pages of the book. He gives life to his words and lays you bare in front of yourself. This book is written in such remarkably simple language that its profound message can easily be understood by all and sundry. It is one of the finest pieces of literature that I have read in my life, an absolute life changer. Let me dissect this masterpiece of literature for you. The next few paragraphs have the power to transform your life for good.

Bertrand Russell has divided this book into two parts where the first part reflects on the reasons behind our sorrow and unhappiness. In the latter part, he gives hope to his readers where he focuses on the things which can actually make us happy. He starts of by giving us eight reasons which make human beings unhappy, namely:

1. Byronic Unhappiness
2. Competition
3. Boredom and Excitement
4. Fatigue
5. Envy
6. Sense of Sin
7. Persecution Mania
8. Fear of Public Opinion

Let's talk first about Byronic unhappiness which is a deep, profound and philosophical concept. In a nutshell, it means Meaninglessness. It is the absence of meaning, purpose or an objective in an individual's life which leads to unhappiness. When humans have dearth of struggle, pursuit, desire and ambition they can go as far as to think that death is better than life. Russell stresses on the fact that effort and struggle towards a worthy ideal in human life is the ultimate guarantee of happiness and ensures contentment.

Russell stresses on the fact that effort and struggle towards a worthy ideal in human life is the ultimate guarantee of happiness and ensures contentment.

Under normal circumstances, we tend to think that less struggle and less effort are tantamount to happiness. A life of prestige and luxury is one in which any hard work is absent and all the privileges of life are free-flowing. Russell rubbishes this concept and proposes that people who get everything easily without any effort do not know what to do in the later part of their lives which promotes their journey towards hollowness and unhappiness. On the other hand, individuals who have identified the purpose of their existence continue to excel despite all odds and find meaning in their journey, which eventually leads them to all the joys of life. A life laced with the pursuit of a worthy ideal is a fulfilling life.

Competition is the second biggest cause of human unhappiness and sadness. Most people compare their success and happiness to that of others, which is where the game goes bad. This feeling of competition does not allow a person to maintain his sanity and peace because he is continuously moving in a vicious cycle of overtaking the person next to him, be they his friends, colleagues or family members. He will have everything that life has to offer but still, he will feel emotionally bankrupt. This person is perennially running on a treadmill where his energy is being wasted, calories are being burnt but he is not getting anywhere. Therefore, if you want to preserve your happiness then stop looking around, be oblivious of the competition and keep on treading your path.

Remember, champions fall in love with boredom. Majority of us do not understand that some level of boredom is important to maintain our mental sanity and equilibrium.

Another very peculiar reason behind unhappiness that has been highlighted by Russell is the absence of boredom. In general, the word boredom tends to carry a negative connotation and we try to avoid this feeling. However, over the last many years I have been a strong advocate of the fact that people who can't stand boredom can never do great things in life. Remember, champions fall in love with boredom. Majority of us do not understand that some level of boredom is important to maintain our mental sanity and equilibrium. Moments when you are not doing anything, are sometimes the best part of your life since they allow you to reflect and think. Hence, it's suggested to bring a pause in your daily juggernaut of life because it can open new avenues of thinking. You need to handle the randomness of your existence in the best possible way.

Another major cause of sadness and anxiety is fatigue (mental and physical). Here we are referring to mental fatigue which is most often caused by unnecessarily thinking about things that are never supposed to happen. You will be amazed to hear that if you just suppress your negative thoughts, more than half of your life worries will cease to exist. Dale

You will be amazed to hear that if you just suppress your negative thoughts, more than half of your life worries will cease to exist.

Carnegie makes a similar point in his book "How to Stop Worrying and Start Living" in which he states that 85% of the worries we have will actually never happen and out of the remaining 15%, almost 79% of the problems can be resolved through little effort. This means, overall 97% of the worries that keep on haunting us are but the products of our wandering mind. Bertrand Russell says that once you think about something, make a decision and then forget about it.

A few of the other sources of unhappiness are envy which is jealousy towards others, sense of sin which means feelings of remorse due to an act which goes against your standard code of conduct and persecution mania which means fear of being reprimanded. Russell also talks about fear of public opinion as one of the biggest causes behind distress in our lives. Whenever you surrender your life to the opinion of others you are bound to be under sheer stress and frustration. Don't seek the approval of the people around you to conduct your life, this is a sure-shot recipe for mental fatigue and anxiety.

Russell also talks about fear of public opinion as one of the biggest causes behind distress in our lives. Whenever you surrender your life to the opinion of others you are bound to be under sheer stress and frustration.

Now let's discuss the reasons which elevate happiness and joy in life. According to Bertrand Russell, happiness has two types: one is "Plain" and the second is "Fancy". He refers to plain happiness as the happiness of the heart and fancy happiness as the happiness of the mind. In his opinion, everyone can achieve plain happiness, it's accessible for all; for example, being first in the race, getting encouragement from a boss or onboarding a big client for your company are all forms of plain happiness. However, fancy happiness is not accessible for all except for those who read and write. Fancy happiness is for people of science, who pursue lifelong learning, gain wisdom and are always in pursuit of learning something new. According to Russell, a scientist is a person who is the happiest individual in the world. This is because he practices what makes him happy

Fancy happiness is not accessible for all except for those who read and write. Fancy happiness is for people of science, who pursue lifelong learning, gain wisdom and are always in pursuit of learning something new.

and makes this practice his profession. This profession not only benefits him but the entire world. This leads to a life of utmost happiness and joy.

One of the prime reasons behind the happiness of people is zest. It is the energy, curiosity and the urge to learn something new all the time. It is the soul of life which helps a person look at various aspects of nature and appreciate them. For a few people the setting of the sun, colours of flowers, colossal mountains and waves of the sea are normal natural phenomena but people who possess zest have the ability to appreciate colours of nature and the ability to understand logic and science underlying these beautiful phenomena. If you want to be happy then create energy within yourself and breed curiosity; it will help you create joy in your life.

Another reason which contributes towards the happiness of people is affection. People who get love, care and respect always remain happy vis-a-vis people who are ignored, specially during childhood. This is dovetailed to a strong family bond whereby children who get maximum attention from their parents develop into happy individuals. Russell strongly criticises the western family system, in which the parents, in the urge to earn more money, tend to ignore their children and when children grow up, they repeat the same act of neglect and put their parents in an old age home. Comparatively, in our part of the world, we still enjoy strong family bonding due to a joint family system. This is the reason why our happiness index compared to the west is still high in spite of limited resources.

If you want to be happy then create energy within yourself and breed curiosity; as it will help you create the joy in your life.

The last thing which I want to discuss about this book is effort and resignation. This means that every human being intrinsically tries to find joy in his work. However, when they fail to achieve anything significant, their life becomes stagnant and meaningless which prompts them to resign from the

efforts of life and find solace in religion. These people resort to religion to justify their existence. Though superficially they might feel happy but deep inside the core of their heart they are unhappy. Therefore, Russell disagrees with this practice and urges his readers to discover the purpose of life and keep striving hard.

This concludes the main postulates of this masterpiece written by a great author. If you ask me, "what makes an individual happy" then I would say it's the continuous pursuit of a progressive ideal in life. There are two important days in a person's life: one is the day he is born and the other is the day when he realises why he is born. Finding your "why" is critical to your well-being, joy and happiness. A rudderless life without effort, struggle and perseverance is usually an unhappy life. Therefore, continue to invest in yourself, strive and achieve the state of self-actualization that helps you justify the purpose of your existence. Once you reach that stage, then in the last part of your life start disseminating whatever you have gathered- your knowledge, intellect, wisdom, fortune and your time. This is a sure shot and time-tested path towards happiness.

Finding your "why" is critical to your well-being, joy and happiness. A rudderless life without effort, struggle and perseverance is usually an unhappy life.

PERSONAL NOTES

Use this space to write your notes and key takeaways from the book.

CONSISTENT IMPROVEMENT EVERY DAY IS THE KEY TO SUCCESS

THE COMPOUND EFFECT
Author: Darren Hardy
Genre: Self-help

Let's start the discussion with an interesting story. Read it meticulously because a big secret of success is hidden in the essence of this story.

Once upon a time, there were two friends, Adnan and Tariq. Adnan possessed a growth mindset and always tried to learn new things. Whatever mistakes he used to commit every day, he used to write them down so that he doesn't repeat them. This practice ensured that his personality evolves as time passed by. Tariq on the other hand possessed a sharp mind and was very intelligent and talented. Due to his intrinsic qualities, he didn't have to put much effort into learning anything new.

The only difference between the two friends is that Adnan believed in daily and consistent learning while Tariq, due to his fixed mindset, mostly relied on making use of his existing skills despite possessing quicker learning skills. As they grow up and reach adulthood, time comes to opt for a job. Each of them is given two choices. There is one job in which the compensation per month is one lakh rupees while the second job provides only one thousand rupees per week. Moreover, in the one lakh rupees job there is no need for daily learning. If you feel like learning any new skills its fine but if you are not interested in evolving, then its ok; there will be no impact on your job status. While in the job worth a thousand rupees a week, learning something daily is mandatory. If this condition is met, it will result in a 10% increase in the existing salary every week. Tariq immediately opts for the high-paying job while Adnan, who believes in lifelong learning, accepts the low-paying job of Rs.1000/week.

The only difference between the two friends is that Adnan believed in daily and consistent learning while Tariq, due to his fixed mindset, mostly relied on making use of his existing skills despite possessing quicker learning skills.

After the end of the first month, Tariq has Rs. 1 lakh while Adnan earns only Rs. 4,641. After six months, Tariq has earned Rs. 600,000 while Adnan has earned only Rs. 88,497. Adnan's friends and relatives make a laughing stock of him and curse him for his decision to opt for such a low-paying job. They often can be heard saying, "What is the use of your learning? See how great Tariq is doing and earning so well. You are wasting your time in learning new skills while the world is moving ahead of you." One year passes by and Tariq has earned 12 lakhs while Adnan has earned Rs. 960,172. If you observe this time, the gap between the two incomes has shrunk.

Eighteen months pass by and a strange phenomenon happens. Tariq, who has been leading for so many months, has accumulated 18 lakh rupees while Adnan has earned a phenomenal amount close to 95 lakh rupees. Let's stretch it further, after completion of two years, Tariq has an accumulated income of Rs 24 lakh while Adnan has earned a whopping Rs 95 Million. This is absolutely jaw dropping. It is not a miracle that has enabled Adnan to come from behind and grow exponentially, rather these are the wonders of the compound effect.

Achieving success requires building momentum instead of quick fixes and shortcuts which intrinsically do not possess longevity.

This is the same effect that Einstein spoke highly about and said, "Compound effect is like the eighth wonder of the world." Darren Hardy has written a remarkable book highlighting this concept with the title "The Compound Effect." Let's discuss some of the remarkable and life-changing concepts in this book, a few of which I practice regularly in my life.

The essence of the compound effect is that to achieve success we should focus on long-term dedication, commitment and self-improvement instead of seeking immediate results; small choices lead to big results. Achieving success requires building momentum instead of quick fixes and shortcuts which intrinsically do not possess longevity. Einstein exclaimed that "I think and think for months and years, 99 times the conclusion is false the 100th time

I am right." Persistence eventually leads a person to success in life.

If you surrender your existence to your fate then chances of excelling are bleak. Therefore, take your life into your own hands and carve your future yourself. Luck happens when preparation meets opportunity. Darren Hardy, through this book, has communicated that steady progress on a daily basis is much better than short bursts of brilliance here and there. For instance, instead of working out for 20minutes every day you pull in a 2-hour workout on one day of the week thinking that it will compensate for the remaining days. This approach does not work. Instead, if you consistently make your healthy behaviour part of your routine you tend to fall into a natural consistent rhythm which makes you unstoppable.

Another key learning from this book are the methods which can help you overcome your bad habits. The modus operandi is as follows. Make a list of your bad habits, like smoking, spending time on mobile and social media, procrastination, etc. Once the list has been made, pick up one habit at a time and start eliminating it from your life. Make a plan, give yourself a deadline and then be steadfast come what may.

A man is known by the associations he has. Therefore, always look to befriend those people from whom you can learn. Work closely with people who push you to grow and achieve greater heights. Do not waste your time with people who do not align with your vision in life and are always ready to belittle and degrade you.

I have made these learnings an integral part of my life since a very long time now and have seen miraculous results. I urge all of you to pay heed to all the recommendations mentioned in the book so you can kick-start your journey towards success.

WE SPEND 33% OF OUR ENTIRE LIVES SLEEPING

WHY WE SLEEP
Author: Matthew Walker
Genre: Psychology

The average age of an individual in our country is between 67-69 years. If we round this off, then on average every Pakistani has a life span of 70 years. Suppose, a person's age is 70 years and he sleeps for 8 hours daily. Simple number crunching reveals that in 70 years of his life, one individual will sleep about 204,400 hours which if converted into years will make 23.3 years. This means that almost 33% of life is spent sleeping. That's a huge number which suggests that sleep is an indispensable and integral part of our life. If any book explains this phenomenon to the core, then it is "Why We Sleep" by Matthew Walker. It is a path-breaking book that provides comprehensive information on the following facets pertaining to sleep:

- What causes us to sleep
- Types of sleep
- How many hours should we sleep
- What are dreams
- Why do we see dreams
- Sleep disorders
- Diseases associated with sleep

Suppose a person's age is 70 years and he sleeps for 8 hours daily. Simple number crunching reveals that in 70 years of his life one individual will sleep about 204,400 hours which if converted into years will make 23.3 years.

I was absolutely flabbergasted after reading this commendable book and realised the importance of sleep in our lives. This book has given me one of the greatest learnings in life and I want to share this learning with all of you. Let's get started.

Matthew Walker is a sleep scientist who has done extensive research on the natural phenomena of sleep for the past 20 years. You will not find many books on this topic but this path-breaking book has decoded the mystery of sleep once and for all. Let's first explore how our body gets to know that it's time to sleep. This happens due to the circadian rhythm which is the biological clock of our body. It tells our body when to sleep and when to wake up. The suprachiasmatic nucleus is the principal circadian clock of the brain which regulates our 24 hours. Another major factor that pushes us to sleep is sleep pressure. While we are awake, a chemical called adenosine builds up in our brain which keeps on increasing in quantity during the time we are awake. This increase is directly proportional to our desire for sleep, that is why it is known as sleep pressure. You must have observed that when you take tea or coffee, especially later in the day, you often tend to lose the urge to sleep. This happens because the caffeine in tea or coffee decreases the effect of this chemical adenosine, leading to distorted sleep habits.

Let's talk about types of sleep now, a really interesting topic. There are fundamentally two types of sleep a) Rapid Eye Movement (REM) and b) Non-Rapid Eye Movement (NREM). NREM has further four stages as well. When we sleep, a war happens between both forms of sleep. Sleep starts with the NREM stage and moves into the REM stage which is also known as deep sleep. During the time we are asleep we keep oscillating between the two types. During the Rapid Eye Movement stage, our eyes move very swiftly. It is at this stage that we witness dreams during our sleep.

The body uses NREM sleep to repair itself, regrow tissues, build bone structure and make the immune system stronger. REM sleep helps us to improve our memory and learning.

There are several advantages of NREM and REM sleep. The body uses NREM sleep to repair itself, regrow tissues, build bone structure and make the immune system stronger. REM sleep helps us to improve our memory and learning. In infants, it contributes to brain development as well. Sleeping 8 hours a day helps us to prolong our life and helps the brain to restore its functions due to which it stays healthy. Always remember to have a good sleep before and after a big learning session since it helps

Sleeping 8 hours a day helps us to prolong our life and helps the brain to restore its functions due to which it stays healthy.

you store and retrieve all that you have learnt. Apart from this, sleep also makes us more creative and attractive. An appropriate amount of sleep helps us to reduce our food cravings which in turn keeps a check on our food consumption patterns and weight.

Sleep also protects us from many ruthless diseases such as Cancer, Dementia, Heart Attack, Diabetes, Anxiety, Depression, Panic Disorder, Bipolar Disorder, etc. Moreover, an amazing function of sleep is its potency to help us in forgetting painful events of life. Sleep has a filtering mechanism that continuously cleans our mind due to which we forget the unwanted memories.

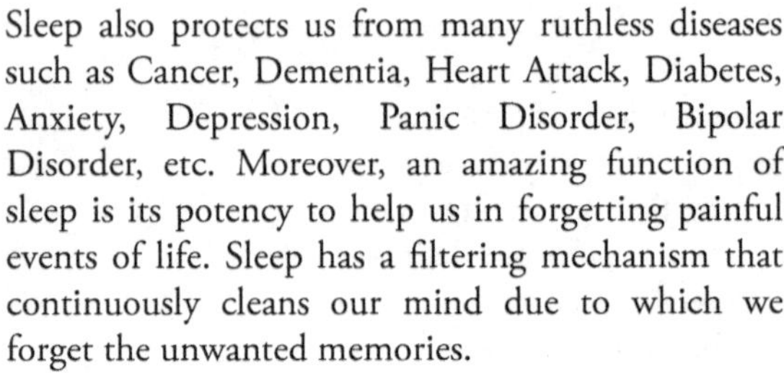

An appropriate amount of sleep helps us to reduce our food cravings which in turn keeps a check on our food consumption patterns and weight.

Dreams are directly dovetailed to our sleep, so let's try to understand their purpose in our life. According to Matthew Walker, dreams act as therapy for us. Dreams help us in improving our emotional, mental and cognitive health. Lucid dreaming helps us in creativity and problem-solving. It is a very unique form of dream in which the individual knows that he is witnessing a dream, therefore, he can control its content as well. This ensures that our mental equilibrium is maintained.

There are several disorders associated with sleep as well. The first is Somnambulism, in which a person suffers from sleep walking, sleep talking and sleep eating. It's such a lethal disorder that sometimes people commit murder as well during sleep (case of Kenneth Paul). Another sleep disorder is Insomnia which is the inability to sleep. In fatal insomnia, a person does not sleep for many months due to which his body functions start collapsing and eventually that person dies. Another strange disorder is Narcolepsy which is the opposite of Insomnia. Narcolepsy leads to massive drowsiness, laziness, and sudden sleep attack even during the daytime. People who suffer from this disorder cannot stay awake for more than a few hours due to which their daily life is severely

handicapped. Two symptoms of this disorder are Cataplexy which is the weakening of muscles leading to slurred speech, and sleep paralysis in which a person becomes temporarily paralysed before going to bed and immediately after waking up.

The book also highlights the biggest impediments to our sleep, one of them is the white LED lighting emitted by our electronic gadgets. These white lights severely disturb our natural clock leading to disintegrated sleep. To have a good night's sleep, shun your access towards all electronic gadgets at least a couple of hours before your sleep. Apart from this, stick to a sleep schedule. Go to bed and wake up at the same time each day. When your body will start following a routine your sleep pattern will automatically improve. Avoiding caffeine and nicotine that we consume via tea, coffee, cola, chocolates and cigarettes helps us in improving our sleep patterns. You can also improve your sleep by inducting 30 minutes of exercise into your daily routine. Avoid consuming a large meal in the latter part of the day since it leads to indigestion which causes disturbed sleep. A dark, cool and gadget-free bedroom can help improve the quality of your sleep as well.

This book was one of my best reads for 2021. It enlightened me about a biological process that we usually do not pay heed to. This is something that I absolutely love about Western authors- they dedicate their entire life in search of finding answers to their curious questions. They tend to pick up a basic and fundamental issue and then decode it thoroughly in great detail. This curiosity to know and the urge for lifelong learning is what has made them leaders of the world. If we are not willing to emulate the West then at least we can build the same sense of curiosity in our nation which may help us look at things beyond the obvious.

An amazing function of sleep is its potency to help us in forgetting painful events of life. Sleep has a filtering mechanism that continuously cleans our mind due to which we forget the unwanted memories .

Avoid consuming a large meal in the latter part of the day since it leads to indigestion which causes disturbed sleep. A dark, cool, and gadget-free bedroom can help improve the quality of your sleep as well.

PERSONAL NOTES

Use this space to write your notes and key takeaways from the book.

FOR LEADERS IT IS ALWAYS PEOPLE FIRST

LEADERS EAT LAST
Author: Simon Sinek
Genre: Business Management

In the world of management sciences, one debate is very common: for an organisation to be successful, should it have good managers or good leaders? There is a lot of polarity on the answer to this question but one thing is for sure, it always has to be a blend of both. You must have seen some cut-outs or placards on the desks of your colleagues where comparison is drawn between a manager and a leader. The fundamental difference between a manager and a leader is that a manager focuses on work while a leader always focuses on people, their professional development, nourishment, growth and progress.

A lot of individuals turn out to be great managers but they do not possess the qualities required to be a leader. They may deliver their work diligently but their team is not synchronised with them and won't miss any opportunity to leave them in the doldrums when the time comes. Most of the companies give the title of leader to their managers assuming that they will transform their employees into superstar performers. This usually doesn't happen because leaders are few and with different personalities. You can't develop every individual into a leader. I am not saying that people are born leaders but there has to be some natural flair which, when backed by the required set of learning, develops an individual into an effective leader.

There have been innumerable books written on the discipline of leadership. One book that is my personal favourite is "Leaders Eat Last" by Simon Sinek. This book enlightens the readers on the art of leadership and how it can transform organisations. The central

The central theme of the book revolves around the circle of safety created by leaders around their employees. It is a very humane and interesting concept.

theme of the book revolves around the circle of safety created by leaders around their employees. It is a very humane and interesting concept.

Simon Sinek says that every individual or employee who works for an organisation is a son or a daughter. When parents send their children for work, deep inside they expect them to receive the same love and care that they have given to their children. This is where the role of a business leader begins, in fact, this is what it means to be a leader. He is like a parent who gives every employee in his company as much love, care and protection as he gives to his own family. Simon Sinek calls this "Circle of Safety." In an organisation employees go through a roller coaster of emotions such as intimidation, humiliation, isolation and rejection; the role of a leader is to reduce such threats and make people comfortable at work by creating synergy in the team. In order to accomplish all this, the leader should possess profound understanding of human psychology. He should have different tools and techniques in his repertoire which will allow him to manage different people in different ways. If you are not good with people you might have a chance of becoming a good manager but there is absolutely no chance of becoming a good leader.

During the global economic crisis in the year 2008, a company named Barry-Wehmiller was severely affected. It lost several high revenue contracts resulting in severe losses. It was inevitable that the CEO of the company, Bob Chapman, had no choice but to let the people go. However, Chapman was a leader; to him, his employees were not ordinary people but like his own family. In his company's conference room, he said some historic words.

"We would never dream of getting rid of one of our children in hard times. If anything, it's better if we all suffer a little so that none of us has to suffer a lot."

After the meeting, instead of laying off people, he introduced a mandatory furlough program in the company, according to which every employee will go on 4 weeks of unpaid leave. Hearing this, the employees who were petrified about the security of their job were so relieved that they steered the company out of hot waters and set a new example. This example of Chapman is a classical representation of the Circle of Safety. When a leader creates a secure and cohesive environment then trust and cooperation between people increases. This leads to organisations achieving great feats. On the other hand, a company with a dearth of high-quality leaders, results in a state of anxiety, confusion, frustration and indecisiveness. In these sorts of cultures, people are detached and selfish and work for themselves rather than for the greater good of the organisation.

When a leader creates a secure and cohesive environment then trust and cooperation between people increases. This leads to organisations achieving great feats.

Another important aspect that Simon Sinek highlights in this book is that a leader must make a personal connection with his people. This will help him in creating the camaraderie that is needed for the employees to be satisfied which in turn helps the company grow as well. The better grip a leader has on the motivations, fears and desires of his people the better he is able to deal with them. This will also assist in leading by trust and competence rather than through title and authority.

Another important aspect that Simon Sinek highlights in this book is that a leader must make a personal connection with his people.

There are several myths and debates about the qualities of a good leader with a large portion of the population believing that a leader is someone who is sincere, honest, dedicated, committed and competent. All these attributes by default should be present in every individual. No big deal. According to me, the biggest quality a leader should possess is the ability to produce more leaders. If a leader is not able to create a team of successors during his tenure, then he doesn't deserve to be given this prestigious title. It is one of the biggest responsibilities of a

According to me, the biggest quality a leader should possess is the ability to produce more leaders. If a leader is not able to create a team of successors during his tenure, then he doesn't deserve to be given this prestigious title.

leader to produce a team of fine individuals who can run the show once his career comes to a twilight. A practical example of this is the legendary Steve Jobs who nominated Tim Cook as his successor during his lifetime. After the death of Jobs, Tim Cook took Apple to even greater heights. I urge all of you to find and observe people around you who possess leadership skills; associate with these people so you can learn directly from them the traits which set individuals apart.

PERSONAL NOTES

Use this space to write your notes and key takeaways from the book.

NEVER

OUTSHINE

YOUR

MASTER

THE 48 LAWS OF POWER
Author: Robert Greene
Genre: Psychology

There are a handful of books in every era which become immortal due to their path-breaking content. The impact of these books is so great that year after year people keep reading them and quote them as references. One such book which falls in this category is "The 48 Laws of Power" by Robert Greene. It is an international bestseller which made Greene an international celebrity. It primarily speaks on the controversial topic of power and influence. Robert Greene can be considered a modern-day Machiavelli because he goes deep inside the labyrinths of human nature, picks up the darkest aspect of man's psychology and pens it down. That is the reason why a lot of people think that this book promotes deceit, cunningness, and shrewdness.

Robert Greene can be considered a modern-day Machiavelli because he goes deep inside the labyrinths of human nature, picks up the darkest aspect of man's psychology and pens it down.

The central idea of the book is that due to certain actions of an individual, his power, grip and control over people can either increase or lose its value. If you see life objectively then it's all a game of power where each and every one of us is part of a power struggle either directly or indirectly. Robert Greene puts forward 48 laws in this book that can help us to boost our spectrum of influence and keep people under control. Let's have a closer look at each one of them.

Law # 1
"Never outshine your master"
Always make those who are above you feel bigger and superior. Exposing your intelligence and intellect pompously in front of your master can create fear and insecurity in him which can go against you. Always make your master feel that he is better than you.

Exposing your intelligence and intellect pompously in front of your master can create fear and insecurity in him which can go against you.

Law # 2

"Never put too much trust in friends, learn how to use enemies"

Don't blindly trust your friends because they will be the first to envy and deceive you. Instead, learn from your enemies because they will always keep you alert.

Law # 3

"Conceal your Intentions"

Keep your intentions secret and hide them from people so that no one can defend himself against you. Keep people confused and walk quietly on your way.

Law # 4

"Always say less than necessary"

Don't lose the importance of your words by talking too much. Keep your words and expressions under control and only speak when necessary.

Keep your words and expressions under control and only speak when necessary.

Law # 5

"So much depends on reputation, guard it with your life"

Your reputation, status and identity are the biggest source of your power. Take good care of them. It's uncompromisable.

Law # 6

"Court attention at all costs"

Make yourself prominent and attract people. Out of sight is out of mind. However, be careful not to attract unnecessary attention all the time. Maintain balance.

Law # 7

"Get others to do the work for you, but always take the credit"

This is vicious. Instead of working yourself make people work and take advantage of their intelligence but when it comes to taking the credit make sure that you swallow all the credit yourself. These are

some of the controversial postulates which make this book so notorious.

Law # 8

"Make other people come to you, use bait if necessary"

Deceive your opponent in a way that he leaves his position and agrees to do whatever you tell him to do. This way you can easily beat him.

Law # 9

"Win through your action, never through argument"

If you want to win over people on your side then do it through action rather than debate. This will be the real victory. Be biased towards action.

If you want to win over people on your side then do it through action rather than debate. This will be the real victory.

Law # 10

"Avoid the unhappy or the unlucky"

Stay away from people who are unhappy and unfortunate in life, since they can also infect you with their misfortune. Vicious!

Law # 11

"Learn to keep people dependent on you"

Don't teach a lion how to climb a tree. Never make people learn so much that they lose dependency on you and become independent. Keep your position solid and relevant.

Law # 12

"Use selective honesty and generosity to disarm your victim"

Don't be honest all the time. Speak the truth only when it is required and works in your favour. Manipulate people through selective deeds at selective occasions.

Don't be honest all the time. Speak the truth only when it is required and works in your favour.

Law # 13

"When asking for help, appeal to people's self-interest, never to their mercy or gratitude"

Whenever you need help from someone don't ask for

a favor or help. Extend your call for help in a way that it's laced with some benefit for the other party as well.

Law # 14
"Pose as a friend, work as a spy"
Show yourself as a friend and act like a spy. This will help you understand the weaknesses and strengths of your opponent.

Law # 15
"Crush your enemy totally"
Eliminate your enemy completely; don't leave any life in him so that any chances of revival are suppressed.

Law # 16
"Use absence to increase respect and honor"
Being available all the time reduces your respect, honour and dignity. Limit your presence so people start to value you.

Law # 17
"Keep others in suspended terror, cultivate an air of unpredictability"
Always confuse people so that they do not understand your behaviour. Keep an element of surprise in all your interactions.

Law # 18
"Do not build fortresses to protect yourself, isolation is dangerous"
Build your team of associates and friends and shun isolation. This will help you in your tough times.

Build your team of associates and friends and shun isolation. This will help you in your tough times.

Law # 19
"Know who you're dealing with, do not offend the wrong person"
Learn the art of dealing with different people in different ways. You should have all the tricks in your repertoire to charm various sets of people. Do not offend or hurt the feelings of such individuals who

can take revenge on you.

Law # 20

"Do not commit to anyone"
Never give people your unconditional support. Do not make them feel that they possess you. If you are fully committed to one side you will lose power over other people.

Never give people your unconditional support. Do not make them feel that they possess you.

Law # 21

"Play a sucker to catch a sucker, seem dumber than your mark"
Sometimes it is good to come across as a fool and show less intelligence in front of your opponents. This will keep them relaxed while you will continue to do what you have to do.

Sometimes it is good to come across as a fool and show less intelligence in front of your opponents.

Law # 22

"Use the surrender tactic: transform weakness into power"
Sometimes surrendering to the circumstances is the first step towards success. If your opponent is strong, work with him and wait patiently for his strength to weaken. Make surrender a tool of power.

Law # 23

"Concentrate your forces"
Improve your strength over time and focus on your strengths through which you can reap maximum benefit.

Law # 24

"Play the perfect courtier"
Be a good courtier, a person who knows all the rules and regulations of the court and who has all kinds of skills. Whoever does that will get the best position eventually.

Law # 25

"Recreate yourself"
In my point of view, this law is the most potent

amongst all other laws. It means that don't blindly accept the role society wants you to play. Find your identity by yourself since you are the owner of your image and reputation.

Law # 26
"Keep your hands clean"
This is again vicious and evil. Whenever anything goes wrong, pass the buck. Don't let your involvement be seen in anything that goes wrong. By the way, in our part of the world, 90% of the people always pass on the responsibility to someone else. Success has many fathers, while failure is an orphan.

Law # 27
"Play on people's need to believe to create a cult-like following"
This is really interesting. It means that in order to win the blind trust of people and create a stream of ardent followers, always use tactics to stimulate their emotions instead of their minds. This is a common modus operandi of religious leaders where they play with the sensitive emotions of people to create a cult following.

Law # 28
"Enter action with boldness"
Whenever you do a task, do it with great passion and bravery. If you have doubts regarding any task then don't do it. If you work with cowardice, the result will also be terse.

Law # 29
"Plan all the way to the end"
The end of any task is very important so execute everything with a plan so that you keep yourself future-proof. The more time you spend on planning, the fewer unwanted surprises you will get.

Law # 30
"Make your accomplishments seem effortless"

The hardwork behind your success and achievements should look effortless.

Law # 31

"Control the options, get others to play with the cards you deal"

Trap people with such options in which in either case you are victorious. They will superficially feel that they are in control but it is actually you who will be calling the shots.

Law # 32

"Play to people's fantasies"

Do not tell people the truth because truth or reality is often bitter and ugly. Life intrinsically for most of the people is already very difficult therefore, take them to an imaginary world where they are kings and queens. A place where all their desires are fulfilled. This trick is very commonly used by Bollywood movies.

Law # 33

"Discover each man's thumbscrew"

Every man has a weakness, find that weakness and use it to your benefit.

Always dress your best and to impress. You yourself will feel elevated when you dress well.

Law # 34

"Be royal in your fashion: Act like a king to be treated like one"

This is one of my favourites. Always carry yourself as royals or kings. If your appearance is shabby then you will be treated accordingly. Always dress your best and impress. You yourself will feel elevated when you dress well.

Law # 35

"Master the art of timing"

Never rush because it shows that you are not in control. Work with patience and forbearance. Develop the ability to have control over time.

Law # 36

"Disdain things you cannot have; ignoring them is the best revenge"
Ignore all the things in life which you cannot afford or achieve. This will help you focus more on attainable objectives.

Ignore all the things in life which you cannot afford or achieve. This will help you focus more on attainable objectives.

Law # 37

"Create compelling spectacles"
In order to increase your power, pretense is necessary. It can be in the form of a big car, an expensive watch, a big house, a big party or jewellery. People get impressed by all these things and easily get influenced by you. Therefore, make symbolism part and parcel of your life.

Law # 38

"Think as you like but behave like others"
Don't show your intelligence or your unconventional ideas to people because they will misunderstand you. It's better and safer to get along with people and blend with them. Only share your original and unique ideas with those friends who can digest them.

Don't show your intelligence or your unconventional ideas to people because they will misunderstand you.

Law # 39

"Stir up waters to catch fish"
Control your anger and emotions and stay calm. However, if you stay composed yourself and make your enemy angry then there is nothing better than that. By doing this you can easily defeat them.

Law # 40

"Despise the free lunch, there is nothing free in life"
Avoid free offers because by doing so you will liberate yourself from obligations. Instead be generous and lion-hearted, since it's a sign of power.

Avoid free offers because by doing so you will liberate yourself from obligations.

Law # 41

"Avoid stepping into a great man's shoes"
If your ancestors were influential, powerful, and famous then do not live your life under their shadow.

Do not repeat what they have already accomplished because to make a name for yourself in their chosen field you have to work twice as hard. Therefore, find new avenues to carve out your identity.

Law # 42

"Strike the shepherd and the sheep will scatter"
Behind every evil, there is always a strong and powerful person. Avoid that person at all costs because he can easily influence everyone negatively and inflict damage upon you.

Law # 43

"Work on the heart and minds of others"
Don't intimidate people. Play with their psychology and gradually seduce and trick them into doing what you want them to do.

Law # 44

"Disarm and infuriate with the mirror effect"
Do the same to your enemy as he does to you. Make them feel like you share the same values. Doing so will prevent them from knowing your strategy and the victory will be yours.

Law # 45

"Preach the need for change but never reform too much at once"
This is a very important point. Whenever people acquire a position of authority, they tend to disregard all the former practices and label them as bad. Don't be too outrageously extreme in this, since it will make people defensive. If you have to change anything, then do it slowly and gradually.

Law # 46

"Never appear too perfect"
Don't become so perfect that people start envying you. Every person has some weaknesses and defects. Own them and in fact, reveal them to the world so they can relate to you and do not consider you an outlier.

Law # 47

"Do not go past the mark you aimed for: In victory, learn when to stop"

Success is intimidating and makes even the best of people arrogant. Such people do not sustain their success for long and fall back to their original position. Don't get carried away by the excitement of success. When you achieve your target stop right there so you do not attract unwanted attention.

Success is intimidating and makes even the best of people arrogant. Such people do not sustain their success for long and fall back to their original position.

Law # 48

"Assume formlessness"

Everything in life changes and evolves over time. That is why it is said that change is the only constant. Keep your pace up with the changing times and always show the flexibility to change. Don't be fixated by a thought or an ideology. Be fluid like water.

Don't be fixated by a thought or an ideology. Be fluid like water.

These were all the laws of this masterpiece. In my personal opinion, I find 70% of these laws to be pragmatic and based on reality. We cannot always hide behind positive virtues because life is not lived in black and white. Always remember that "It is the mark of an educated mind to be able to entertain a thought without accepting it." This means that it is not always necessary that whatever is being told to you resonates with your personal thought process.

You should have the maturity of mind to accept or reject a thought based on thorough analysis. There are always various angles to look at anything. You should be aware of the narrative and counter-narrative, this will help you formulate your opinions in the best possible way.

PERSONAL NOTES

Use this space to write your notes and key takeaways from the book.

LOW
PREDICTABILITY,
HIGH IMPACT

THE BLACK SWAN
Author: Nassim Nicholas Taleb
Genre: Philosophy

On June 30, 2018, an unimaginable incident took place in Burari, Delhi. A seemingly happy Bhatia family committed collective suicide. All 11 members of the family hung themselves from the ceiling of the house, ending their lives in a matter of a night. When their small retail store didn't open as usual in the early morning, their neighbour, Gurcharan Singh, became curious and went to their house to inquire if all was well. He tried knocking many times but with no response so he opened the door and got the shock of his life. He saw the bodies of the entire Bhatia family hanging from the ceiling like a Banyan tree. Upon investigation, it was revealed that one member of the family, named Lalit, suffered from delusional disorder. Lalit seemingly used to hear the voice of his dead father who used to pass on instructions on how to conduct life which he used to convey to the entire family. The whole family trusted Lalit and saw him as the head of the family. Therefore, they had no other option but to adhere to all that he had to say. During one of these delusional episodes, he instructed the entire family to hang from the ceiling as a religious ritual that ended up in costing them their lives.

The purpose of telling this story is to discuss a remarkable book and its unusual concept which revolves around the importance of outliers and unpredictability in our lives. Nassim Nicholas Taleb is a Lebanese-American author who shot to global fame through his book "The Black Swan" published in 2007. It is the same book that predicted the 2008 financial crisis as well. The bottom line of the book is that we tend to look for logic, reasons and order in our world. We think that with data and information

we can forecast the future but most of the things in our life do not follow logic and pre-defined pattern. Black Swan events are the ones we can't predict and imagine even with the most meticulous analysis. These events have low predictability yet high impact like the aforementioned example of the unusual demise of the Bhatia family which no one could have imagined. Similarly, the rise of Hitler, First World War, 9/11 and most recently the Coronavirus are all such events that fall in the category of Black Swans.

Black Swan events are the ones we can't predict and imagine even with the most meticulous analysis. These events have low predictability yet high impact.

Nassim Taleb writes that before the discovery of Black Swans in Western Australia the whole world used to think that swans are white. However, as soon as Black Swans were discovered, their entire identity was changed. The underlying logic and philosophy behind this book is that we tend to believe that we know everything about the world but in reality, our lives are shaped by events that are outrageous and unforeseen. Let's discuss some critical points from the book.

The underlying logic and philosophy behind this book is that we tend to believe that we know everything about the world but in reality, our lives are shaped by events that are outrageous and unforeseen.

Nassim Taleb writes that our life is actually a black swan event since most of the major events in our lives like meeting your spouse, career, etc. happened to us without any formal planning. Black Swan logic states that it is the unexpected that shapes our lives. The things that we don't know are much more important as compared to what we know; therefore, it's better that instead of confirming our existing ideas we should try to falsify them. This means that whenever we try to predict the future, we need to critique our existing information and look for outliers that no one would have thought about.

Black Swan logic states that it is the unexpected that shapes our lives. The things that we don't know are much more important as compared to what we know.

A black swan event has three characteristics. Firstly, "it is an outlier" which means it deviates from the norm. The second identity of black swan events is that they have low predictability yet high impact especially negative black swan events like Earthquakes, 9/11, Coronavirus, etc. The third sign

A black swan event has three characteristics. Firstly, "it is an outlier" which means it deviates from the norm.

of black swan events is that they are only explainable after the impact. This is why they are also referred to as the Problem of Induction which means an event that is hard to justify and explain rationally. Nassim Taleb states that after so much progress in science and technology, we tend to overestimate the extent of our knowledge and think that we can decode any phenomenon but that's not true.

He calls it the Triplet of Opacity in which the first point is "False Understanding" where we believe that we understand most of what is going on in the world but things, in reality, are quite different from our understanding. The second point is "Retrospective Distortion" which means that we associate a story with an event once it has happened and refer to it as history. The third point is "Overvaluing facts, statistics and categories" where we rely on facts and logic to explain the science behind things but the big impact events elude any sort of analysis.

In our universe, most of the impactful events never follow a linear path, rather they are outliers. These events suddenly show up leaving us unprepared and startled. Nassim Taleb also states a controversial thing here where he disregards any proper planning and design behind major scientific inventions. He refers to all major scientific inventions as a product of a black swan event. The best example in support of this argument is that of Alexander Graham Bell, the gentleman who invented the telephone. Graham Bells' mother was deaf and he had a desire to invent a device through which he could help his mother revive her sense of hearing. After innumerable hits and misses, instead of developing a hearing aid, he ended up inventing the first telephone accidentally. Another example of a black swan is the research and development which happens in the pharmaceutical industry where a lot of medicines are discovered by chance. Nassim values randomness a lot and he made this unpredictability the topic of another book titled

"Fooled by Randomness." It is an amazing book that discusses the hidden role of chance in our lives.

The Black Swan is one of the finest works of modern philosophy. Upon reading this book, you realise how different things can be to what superficially they might seem. Can you identify a Black Swan event in your life?

PERSONAL NOTES

Use this space to write your notes and key takeaways from the book.

IT IS NEVER TOO LATE TO MAKE YOUR BRAIN SHARP AND INTELLIGENT

KEEP SHARP
Author: Dr. Sanjay Gupta
Genre: Psychology

There is a general consensus amongst common people that any human being is born with a certain set of attributes, intellect and IQ which are etched in stone and no further cerebral development is possible. In common culture, we believe in geniuses who are born with a sharp mind and who eventually make it big. However, recent advancements in research regarding our brain have revealed that with the right amount of push, new neural networks can be developed in the brain which can increase our IQ and further boost our cognitive processes. There is never a finish line. You can continue to evolve and grow your mind if you continuously feed it with the right set of inputs.

Our brain has been a source of mystery for scientists, psychologists and philosophers for centuries. In popular culture, some myths about our brain are completely wrong. For instance, human beings use only 5%-10% of their brainpower during their lifetime. After the age of 40, brain processes start deteriorating. Once brain cells are dead, they permanently die down and cannot be replenished. The good news is that we can nurture our brain and make it sharp and perform better.

In the next few paragraphs, I will give you a comprehensive plan to make your brain sharper and more intelligent which will help you lead a quality life, boost your reasoning power, cognitive skills and emotional intelligence.

Dr. Sanjay Gupta is a CNN correspondent and a neurosurgeon who has written a remarkable book

Recent advancements in research regarding our brain have revealed that with the right amount of push, new neural networks can be developed in the brain which can increase our IQ and further boost our cognitive processes. There is never a finish line.

with the name "Keep Sharp" which is a complete treatise on how to make our brain sharp. It includes a 12-week long program to train our brain. Dr. Gupta in the book has frequently referred to dementia as one of the most lethal diseases caused by the brain's deterioration. In this condition, the person starts forgetting things- even his name, his children, the map of his home and his other whereabouts. Dr. Gupta gives us a great framework consisting of five pillars to prevent dementia and various other brain diseases. Let's have a look at these 5 items.

The first of these pillars is "Move" which means exercise to stimulate your body. Regular exercise helps us in boosting our metabolism, digestion, improves body toning, and makes our heart's health better. In addition to all this, regular workouts also make our brain sharp, save us from depression, dementia and also provide emotional stability. He suggests that a person should at least have 5 days of workout every week. In these 5 days, he should primarily conduct cardio exercises like walking, jogging, hiking, cycling, jumping, swimming, etc.

The second pillar is very important and that is "Discover." Our brain is like a map of a country or city in which there are umpteen number of alleys and streets. However, due to our laziness and incompetence, we take the same path all our lives and never discover new avenues of thought. This is called cognitive reserve. A person who is curious and willing to learn, his cognitive reserve will always be on the higher side. These sorts of individuals keep challenging their brain due to which different networks emerge inside their mind which eventually saves them from dementia and other brain diseases.

You can stimulate your brain through the most trivial of activities. For instance, if you hold your toothbrush from the left hand try brushing your teeth through your right hand next time. Similarly, learning new languages enables new networks to emerge in your brain. Moreover, learning a musical instrument helps you discover new real estate in your mind as well.

Next comes "Sleep and Relaxation" which is about the importance of sleep in our lives. Most people think that sleeping is a passive activity but during sleep, our brain works wonders for us. It filters information, improves memory, helps us forget painful events of our lives and builds tissues leading to a much sharper mind. After sleep comes "Food", you all know that our physical health depends on our diet. The better the diet, the healthier and longer life will be. You can make your brain sharper by adding a balanced diet as a part of your lifestyle which will also increase the longevity of your life.

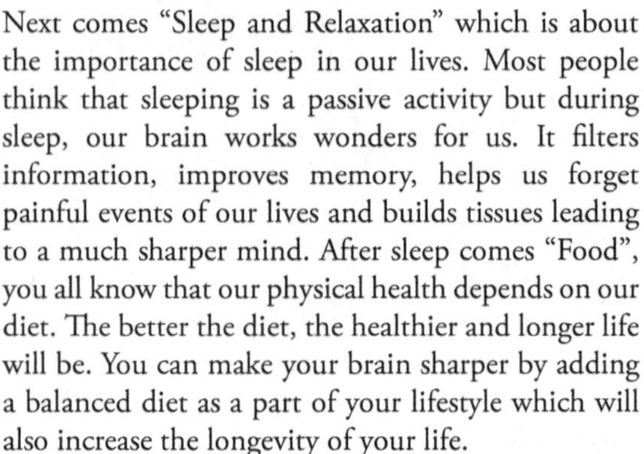

People who have strong family bonding, unconditional support system and strong emotional connection with people live a very fulfilling and happy life.

The fifth and last point is "Connection." Very famous research from Harvard University which has been going on for the last 80+ years has seemed to answer the following question "What makes an individual happy?" After years of analysis and data crunching, it has been understood that neither money nor fame make an individual happy. Rather it is the emotional connection that he builds with people during his lifetime is which contributes to his ultimate happiness. People who have strong family bonding, unconditional support system and strong emotional connection with people live a very fulfilling and happy life.

Dr. Gupta also proposes a 12-week plan to make your brain sharper. Let's review it briefly. In the first two weeks, you have to focus on the five pillars which I have already elaborated. In week three and four kick soft drinks out of your life. Gone are the days of drinking Pepsi, Coke and 7UP. Moreover, try to add fish as part of your diet twice a week. In the fifth and sixth week, you have to kick processed food out of your life and also add fifteen more minutes to

your daily exercise routine. In the seventh and eighth week, you have to start reading and do learning exercises. Spend the ninth and tenth week, asking yourself the following questions:

Am I getting at least thirty minutes of exercise at least five days a week? Am I learning something new that challenges my mind? Am I getting more restful sleep? Am I connected with my friends and family members regularly? In the eleventh and twelfth week, examine what worked and what didn't. Once you do that, keep on treading the same path with commitment and dedication.

This is how according to Dr. Sanjay Gupta you can keep your brain young, sharp and intelligent till your old age. The bottom line is that the cells in our brain can be regenerated and nurtured as opposed to common belief. We have to develop the habit of challenging it every now and then, exercise regularly, read, breed curiosity and focus on positive things in our life.

PERSONAL NOTES

Use this space to write your notes and key takeaways from the book.

A HUMAN BEING CAN POSSESS 8 DIFFERENT TYPES OF INTELLIGENCE

FRAMES OF MIND
Author: Howard Gardner
Genre: Psychology

In general, IQ (intelligence quotient) is considered to be the most potent yardstick to measure human intelligence. You will often see people around you getting impressed by the IQ level of a few individuals. This is because high IQ is superficially directly proportional to the amount of success that an individual will get during his lifetime. However, in the year 1983, Howard Gardner who was a professor of psychology at Harvard University propagated a very unique idea in his book "Frames of Mind."

He stated that IQ testing does measure mathematical or logical intelligence, but it is not a good or effective way to measure human potential. For example, IQ testing is not a useful way to test your talent for composing music, for learning a language, for coding a computer program and for testing your leadership skills. As a result, Gardner proposed different types of intelligence in this book which give you a comprehensive understanding of various forms of intelligence that we possess. According to Gardner, a person is a blend of about eight kinds of intelligence. A few of us possess linguistic intelligence, some have musical intelligence and some have interpersonal. It is our responsibility to discover which form of intelligence we possess and how we can make the best use of it. Let's have a look at all of them.

IQ testing is not a useful way to test your talent for composing music, for learning a language, for coding a computer program and for testing your leadership skills.

Linguistic intelligence comes first. This intelligence is about a person's language skills. People with sharp linguistic intelligence learn different languages very quickly and convince people very easily through the use of language. People who possess refined linguistic intelligence become great storytellers, writers, poets,

People with sharp linguistic intelligence learn different languages very quickly and convince people very easily through the use of language.

journalists, lawyers and politicians. A few of the famous people who had supreme linguistic skills were Adolf Hitler, Martin Luther King, Zulfiqar Ali Bhutto and Lee Kaun Yew. Therefore, if you think that you have good command over language and can persuade people around you then opt for a profession where you can maximise its use.

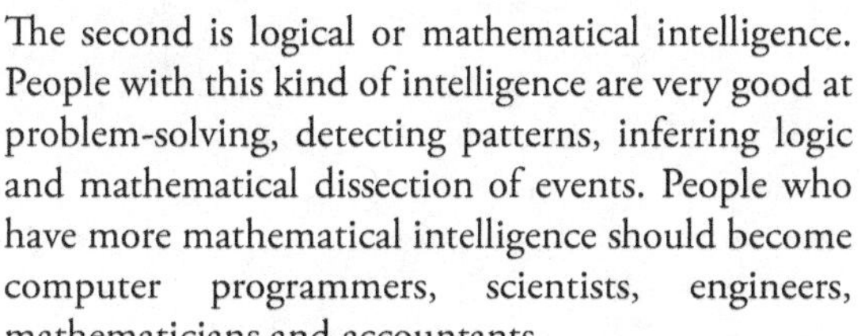

People who have more mathematical intelligence should become computer programmers, scientists, engineers, mathematicians and accountants.

The second is logical or mathematical intelligence. People with this kind of intelligence are very good at problem-solving, detecting patterns, inferring logic and mathematical dissection of events. People who have more mathematical intelligence should become computer programmers, scientists, engineers, mathematicians and accountants.

Next comes musical intelligence. These people pick up patterns of sounds, rhythm and music very well. That is the reason why they become musicians, DJs, singers and composers like Beethoven, Mozart and A.R. Rehman. Another type of intelligence is bodily or kinesthetic intelligence. People who possess strong kinesthetics can coordinate and express their body and physical movements in a very powerful way. For example acrobats, gymnasts and athletes.

The fifth kind of intelligence is very interesting and unique, it's known as visual and spatial intelligence. People with such intelligence understand the placement of any object in space. People with spatial intelligence are masters of decorating houses and make the best use of available space. This is why they often develop themselves as interior designers and architects.

The sixth type of intelligence is interpersonal intelligence. These people are experts in relationship building, are remarkable motivators and have a profound understanding of the psychology of people. Generally, they go on to become salespersons, counsellors, educators and politicians. Usually, business management

The sixth type of intelligence is interpersonal intelligence. These people are experts in relationship building, are remarkable motivators and have a profound understanding of the psychology of people.

students tend to possess interpersonal intelligence.

The seventh form of intelligence is intrapersonal intelligence. These individuals have an excellent process of self-appraisal and remarkable self-awareness. They are aware of their strengths and weaknesses and act accordingly. Writers and Philosophers possess a high level of intrapersonal intelligence.

The last type is naturalistic intelligence. People who possess this form of intelligence are instinctively attracted towards flora and fauna existing in nature. They also find special interest in environmental issues. People with this kind of intelligence enjoy outdoor excursions like hiking, camping, caring for animals, learning about nature, recycling and caring for the environment. Greta Thunberg is a very good example of a human possessing naturalistic intelligence.

This book was an eye-opener for me since it decimated a long-time belief that IQ is the single biggest indicator of the intelligence of an individual. Our education system needs to learn a lot from this extensive research of Gardner. This segregation of different forms of intelligence can serve as the beacon for all people associated with the discipline of education. Our shabby and outdated education model tends to disregard any sort of intelligence which lies outside the realms of the quintessential exam-based education system.

If you are a parent or a teacher and currently reading this then promise yourself that from today onwards you will not impose your opinions and thought process on your child. Let your children fly and discover the strengths of their personalities themselves. Those times are gone when every parent wanted their child to be a doctor or an engineer. In the modern economy, the whole world has

transformed into a global village where individuals have umpteen options to choose their desired field. They can be musicians, bankers, data scientists, athletes, architects, etc. Let them be, whatever they want to be.

If you give your child freedom, liberty and the opportunity to discover the kind of intelligence that they possess then mark my words this will be your biggest contribution to your child's life.

PERSONAL NOTES

Use this space to write your notes and key takeaways from the book.

WHAT MAKES PROPHET MUHAMMAD (PBUH) THE MOST INFLUENTIAL PERSON IN HISTORY?

THE 100
Author: Michael Hart
Genre: Biography/Autobiography

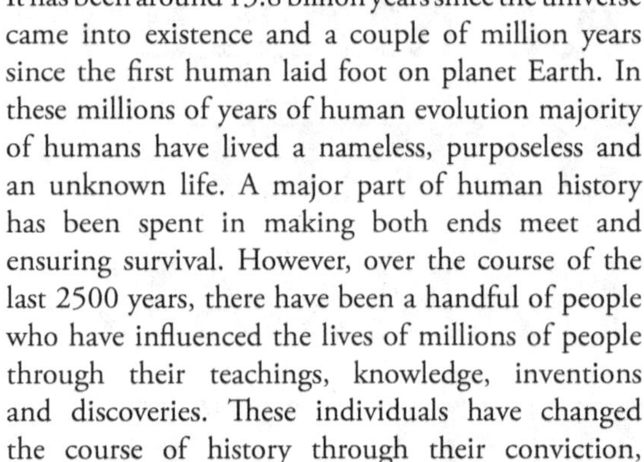

It has been around 13.8 billion years since the universe came into existence and a couple of million years since the first human laid foot on planet Earth. In these millions of years of human evolution majority of humans have lived a nameless, purposeless and an unknown life. A major part of human history has been spent in making both ends meet and ensuring survival. However, over the course of the last 2500 years, there have been a handful of people who have influenced the lives of millions of people through their teachings, knowledge, inventions and discoveries. These individuals have changed the course of history through their conviction, perseverance, determination and intellect. This is the reason why they fall in the category of "influential" people.

In the year 1978, an American scholar, Dr. Michael Hart wrote a book titled "The 100." This book is a ranking of the top 100 most influential personalities in history. It includes individuals from different walks of life like scientists, inventors, political leaders, religious leaders, explorers, businessmen, psychologists, etc. It is a premier list of the most famous individuals the world has ever seen like Aristotle, Plato, Karl Marx, Sigmund Freud, Isaac Newton, Albert Einstein, Napoleon Bonaparte and the list goes on.

There are two interesting facts about this book. The first is that the ranking flows from top to bottom in descending order. This means that Michael Hart has actually numbered people based on how influential they are and then given them rankings in a flow so

the most influential individual occupies number one rank, second most influential number two and the list goes on. The second most important and critical point is that in spite of being a non-Muslim scholar he has given the first rank to Prophet Muhammad (PBUH). This is despite the fact that there are many stalwarts in history like Jesus Christ, Einstein, Newton who the western world regards to be head and shoulders above the rest.

Despite being a non-Muslim scholar he has given the first rank to Prophet Muhammad (PBUH).

Not only has he ranked Prophet Muhammad (PBUH) as the most influential person in history but he has also given solid and concrete reasons to justify it as well. For the Muslim community across the globe which is in excess of 1.9 Billion, this is a matter of great pride and joy. Although the personality of Prophet Muhammad (PBUH) is not dependent on any ranking; however, when a non-Muslim does an objective analysis then his views do hold value.

Michael Hart has a remarkable understanding of western culture and attitude. Therefore, right at the start of the book, he states that a vast majority in the West will be startled and amazed that how can Jesus Christ be replaced with Prophet Muhammad (PBUH) to hold the first rank. To support his argument Professor Hart gives some really concrete reasons. He proclaims that in the long history of our universe Prophet Muhammad (PBUH) is the only leader who achieved astounding and path-breaking success in the discipline of religion as well as politics. No individual has had such a colossal impact on humanity except Prophet Muhammad (PBUH).

He exclaims that in the long history of our universe Prophet Muhammad (PBUH) is the only leader who achieved astounding and path-breaking success in the discipline of religion as well as politics.

Firstly, he founded the religion of Islam in the deserts of Arabia making it one of the most pervasive religions in the world. When the Holy Prophet was born in Mecca in the year 570 AD, it was one of the most underdeveloped regions in the world where people used to follow primitive customs, traditions and cults. There was almost zilch emphasis on education, learning, intellectual development, progress and social development. Amid all this, Holy Prophet spent his childhood as an orphan and lived the life of a common man. During this time, he developed his personality and was recognised as one of the most pious and honest individuals in Arab society. He was a master negotiator and diplomat due to which different clans and tribes used to call him to settle their disputes with their enemies.

At the age of 40, he was bestowed prophethood by the Almighty after which he initiated his struggle to create a community of achievers and leaders. Through his sheer hard work, integrity, perseverance and commitment he achieved the most glorious victories from the tyrants of that era and established Islam as the incumbent religion of the Arab land. After his death, Islam continued to spread and Muslims had major victories in regions of Persia, Syria, Egypt, Europe, and Africa.

At the age of 40, he was bestowed prophethood by the Almighty after which he initiated his struggle to create a community of achievers and leaders.

Most people who are part of the list of "The 100" were born into relatively civilised societies. However, the distinction that Prophet Muhammad (PBUH) had was that despite being born in a regressive society he developed not only himself but also the people around him to create a large community of achievers.

The distinction that Prophet Muhammad (PBUH) had was that despite being born in a regressive society he developed not only himself but also the people around him to create a large community of achievers.

During his lifetime, he was able to create a welfare state in Medina which is considered to be a benchmark of a progressive and prosperous community.

Michael Hart gives a couple of more reasons for placing Prophet Muhammad (PBUH) ahead of Jesus Christ. Although Christians outnumber the Muslims in terms of followers of a particular faith yet Prophet Muhammad's (PBUH) role was much more pivotal and indispensable in the spread of Islam vis-a-vis that of Jesus Christ for Christianity. Although the basic moral principles and tenets of Christianity

were given by Jesus Christ, however, it was developed as a religion by St. Paul, who wrote most of the New Testament himself.

When Prophet Muhammad (PBUH) laid the foundation of Islam, he gave Muslims a comprehensive moral code of conduct to spend their lives. He was bestowed by God the Holy book "Quran Majeed" which is a source of Islamic jurisprudence and provides a beacon for Muslims to conduct their lives in accordance with the orders of Allah and Sunnah of Prophet Muhammad (PBUH). In fact, Michael Hart has said that Prophet Muhammad's influence on Islam is so great that even if the efforts of St. Paul and Jesus Christ are combined, they will fall short. Moreover, from a political point of view as well Prophet Muhammad (PBUH) was very successful. He was an expert diplomat, tactician, negotiator and a mentor for the entire community. Apart from his religious influence, the political impact and influence that he had on Arabia and subsequently on the Islamic world is what makes him the most influential personality in history.

There are many other stalwarts who have been mentioned in the book. You can get to know a lot about their personalities and contributions towards humanity from "The 100."

While reading "The 100" a thought resonated in my mind eventually transforming itself into a question: "How can we leave an impact and be influential in our lives?" I surely have an answer to this question. I am a firm believer in the fact that every human being is born with a certain purpose. During the course of his life, he needs to put in the right effort to discover his "why." The ultimate purpose of life that I always advocate is to develop a community and leave a legacy behind you. Legacy is a word that means, 'Did I matter?' Your personality and life should be crafted in a way where it gives back to the people and

society. Invest in yourself, prepare yourself, acquire knowledge, be financially stable and reach the state of self-actualization as soon as possible. Once you get there, you need to give back whatever you have acquired- your skills, your knowledge, your wealth, your fortune, your experience, your wisdom and your virtues. This is the only way you can be influential during your lifetime and even after you die.

Just do a small thought experiment. Imagine you are on your death bed and about to leave the world. Ask yourself this question: "Am I leaving a better and brighter future for the people around me?" If the answer is no, then something big was missed in your life and if the answer is yes, then you have fulfilled the purpose of your life.

Your personality and life should be crafted in a way where it gives back to the people and society. Invest in yourself, prepare yourself, acquire knowledge, be financially stable and reach the state of self-actualization as soon as possible.

Imagine you are on your death bed and about to leave the world. Ask yourself this question: "Am I leaving a better and brighter future for the people around me?" If the answer is no, then something big was missed in life and if the answer is yes, then you have fulfilled the purpose of your life.

PERSONAL NOTES

Use this space to write your notes and key takeaways from the book.

PERSONAL NOTES

Use this space to write your notes and key takeaways from the book.

TRY TO MAKE ONE ROOM IN YOUR HOUSE AS BEAUTIFUL AS POSSIBLE

BEYOND ORDER
Author: Dr. Jordan Peterson
Genre: Self-help

Four things are very famous about Canada: cold temperatures, Justin Bieber, their current Prime Minister Justin Trudeau and lastly none other than Jordan Peterson. If there is one super star in the world of literature today, it is Jordan Peterson. Dr. Peterson is a clinical psychologist and professor at the University of Toronto who started gaining recognition through his recorded lectures which were published on YouTube. The game changed when he published his magnum opus, 12 Rules for Life which went on to become an international best seller. In the modern world, Jordan Peterson is perhaps the only writer in the world who attracts a global audience due to which his lectures are attended by thousands of people across the globe.

In the year 2021, he published a sequel to his book 12 Rules for Life which was titled "Beyond Order - 12 more rules for life." These rules are a further extension to his 12 rules which again gained worldwide recognition. In the next few paragraphs, I will explain these rules in the simplest manner so you can understand and adopt them as well.

Rule No. 1 is very interesting and it goes like this: "Try to make one room in your house as beautiful as possible." Dr. Peterson believes that beauty is a window into the divine. Anything that is beautiful and in spiritually uplifts you and gives you a chance to think and act better. Everyone tries to decorate their house according to their means but if you can't makeover your entire house then make sure you have a room in it that looks good Gend beautiful. This is an investment not only in your house but in yourself.
The next two rules are relatively similar so we will

cover them together. Rule No. 2 is "Imagine who you could be and then aim single-mindedly at that" while rule No. 3 is "Work as hard as you possibly can on at least one thing and see what happens." These two are what I call in my language life-changing rules. Peterson through these two statements has conveyed the most fundamental objective of life. He encourages to keep some inspiration alive in your life. Set a goal, a target or an objective that you can pursue with passion and obsession. Try to visualise your future and see what you can achieve. There should be at least one thing in your life to which you devote and dedicate yourself because eventually, it will lead you to glory and success. For example, Book Buddy is one of the greatest passions of my life which is driven by the desire to educate and mentally nourish my people through intellectual development. I have always approached this medium through a very transparent and laser-focused approach which has given me tremendous success since I am able to not only connect but influence the lives of my lovely followers.

Rule No. 4 is very interesting, especially for couples and that is "Plan and work diligently to maintain the romance in your relationship." Peterson believes that after marriage the romance between husband and wife takes a back seat and loses its charm. The mind of couples is confounded by the daily hustle of life, nurturing children, family pressure, household budgeting and future planning due to which romance goes out the window. In order to restore this long-lost romance, he suggests that couples should go on a date regularly and spend some exclusive time together. Another fruitful advice that he gives to couples is to have at least 90 minutes of unadulterated conversation in a week. This discussion can revolve around any facet of their life; the important thing is to get the conversation going.

I will dovetail the next two rules as well. Rule No. 5 goes like this: "Do not hide unwanted things in

the fog." Similarly, rule No. 6 is: "If old memories still make you cry, write them down carefully and completely." Dr. Peterson is a clinical psychologist due to which he has an amazing understanding of human psychology. He is fully aware of what is good and what can have an adverse effect on the mental health of individuals. Therefore, he promotes the concept of facing our fears to improve our psychological and emotional wellbeing. He advocates that we should not suppress our fears and painful experiences, rather we should fight them to get rid of them.

Rule No. 7 and 8 are also interrelated so let's read and understand them together: "Be grateful in spite of your suffering" and "Do not allow yourself to become resentful, deceitful or arrogant." Never consider yourself a victim of your circumstances. Even if you are undergoing the toughest of challenges, be grateful for the life that you have. Moreover, never dodge or cheat in life or be arrogant because all these traits eventually lead to failure.

Rule No. 9 is simple and it goes like this: "Do not do things that you hate." Never undertake a task, a profession, or any chore which you abhor since it is equivalent to telling a lie. Although, there might be situations in your life where you are under obligation to do something that you hate, and that is perfectly fine. However, in the long run, stay away from matters with which you are not comfortable.

Rule No. 10 is "Notice that opportunity lurks where responsibility has been abdicated." This is a remarkable rule and my personal favourite. Basically, Dr. Peterson wants us to understand that most people are afraid of hard work and shy away from responsibility. Eventually, regret seeps in and they can only be seen complaining about their missed opportunities. Difficulty and struggle are embedded in the fabric of our life, the sooner you realise it the better it is for you. A large number of people give up only when they are just a few steps away from

success and achievement. Go the extra mile, work extra hard, suffer a little bit more, sacrifice a little bit more, and eventually, you will see the gates of success opening for you.

Rule No. 11 is "Abandon ideology." This means that always be receptive and open to new ideas and avenues of learning instead of being fixated on a one-dimensional ideology-driven mindset. Always be willing to unlearn and relearn, challenge your preconceived notions and your pre-established perceptions about different matters of life. You have to make sure that you always know the narrative and its counter-narrative and once you do then formulate your opinion. This opinion should evolve with time as you learn new dimensions about anything and create new learning pathways in your mind.

Rule No. 12 is "Do not carelessly denigrate social institutions or creative achievements." This means that no matter how rebellious you are and in total disobedience of societal norms, you still have to respect social institutions. While you can continue to explore your personality and life in order to maintain your sanity, you have to keep pace with society and the people around you. This is the reason why he has named this book "Beyond Order" which means that you have to put your one foot in order which moves along the pre-established norms and one foot beyond order so you can continue to grow and evolve.

These are the amazing set of rules which this book propagates. Dr. Peterson is a controversial figure as well due to his strong stance on feminism, patriarchy and other pressing societal matters. What attracts me the most about the professor is his eloquence and strong grip on the language. I think he is the only writer after Bertrand Russell who can give such remarkable expression to his thought. Which rule did you like the most and why?

PERSONAL NOTES

Use this space to write your notes and key takeaways from the book.

STAND UP STRAIGHT WITH YOUR SHOULDERS BACK IS THE FIRST RULE OF SUCCESS

12 RULES FOR LIFE
Author: Dr. Jordan Peterson
Genre: Self-help

A few years ago Dr. Jordan Peterson, Professor of Psychology at the University of Toronto answered a random question on a famous website, Quora. com. The question was, "What are the most valuable things everyone should know"? His answer consisted of 42 postulates which highlighted the important things to do in life. Gradually, his answer became an absolute super hit with millions of people liking and sharing it. Dr. Peterson eventually compressed these 42 principles into 12 rules and wrote a path-breaking book titled "12 Rules For Life." This book catapulted him to superstardom and made him a global thought leader. Let's review the 12 rules of this magnificent piece of literature.

The first amazing rule is "Stand up straight with your shoulders back." This is really succinct and profound. Dr. Peterson explains this rule by connecting human beings to lobsters. He states that there is a dominance hierarchy within lobsters and the ones which have high levels of serotonin have a dominant, upright and confident posture. Due to the excellent posture of a few lobsters, they occupy top positions in the hierarchy. Something similar happens in humans as well. Our societies are also divided into hierarchies when it comes to wealth, fortune and social status. We spend our whole life in the struggle to improve our position in this hierarchy. Standing up straight with your shoulders back means accepting the realities of life with responsibility and having the guts to make it better. This transformation starts with a confident posture. If you slouch and let yourself loose, then life will also give you a lackluster response. However, if you are confident, your posture is straight and

Standing up straight with your shoulders back means accepting the realities of life with responsibility and having the guts to make it better.

you stand tall then not only people but life will also respect and dignify you.

The second rule is "Treat yourself like someone you are responsible for helping." Dr. Peterson states that we care about our pets more than we care about ourselves, that's how we are wired. However, it is indispensable for us to care for ourselves before anything else. Ask yourself this question: "What would my future be like if I started taking care of myself, my learning habits, personality, hygiene and my intellect?" This one question will resolve your major life issues. You can steer your life and choose between heaven or hell. Therefore, understand your responsibility towards yourself and live accordingly.

"What would my future be like if I started taking care of myself, my learning habits, personality, hygiene and my intellect?" This one question will resolve your major life issues.

Rule No. 3 is very simple: "Make friends with people who want the best for you." Always keep association with those people whose friendship you can recommend to your parents and siblings. There is no selfishness in choosing those individuals as friends who are aligned to your vision in life and who support you unconditionally.

Whatever you might achieve in life, no matter what you accomplish there will always be someone who is far more competent and successful than you.

Rule No. 4 is also very meaningful and it goes like this: "Compare yourself to who you were yesterday not who someone else is today." Please make a note of this essential rule for life, especially in today's Instagram-driven world since it is vital for the stability of your mental health. Whatever you might achieve in life, no matter what you accomplish, there will always be someone who is far more competent and successful than you. If you are in a constant state of comparison, you will never be happy. In the race of life, you are playing different roles; family, career and personal. It's not mandatory that you have to win at every game. Remember, "happiness is always found on the journey uphill not in the fleeting sense of satisfaction awaiting at the next peak." If you are better than your yesterday then you are treading the right path.

Remember, "happiness is always found on the journey uphill not in the fleeting sense of satisfaction awaiting at the next peak."

Rule No. 5 is "Do not make your children do anything that makes you dislike them." Dr. Peterson categorically advocates the fact that children should be groomed and nurtured very carefully, especially at an early age so they become socially desirable. When you protect your kids from misadventure and don't allow them to be bold enough to explore, you are stunting their growth. It is the duty of every parent to maximise their child's learning ability and find a balance between fear and pain. Do not put undue pressure on your kids. Let them grow and explore their way through life.

When you protect your kids from misadventure and don't let them be bold enough to explore, you are stunting their growth.

Rule No. 6 is "Set your house in perfect order before you criticise the world." This simply means that before you start preaching to the world superior moral values and code of conduct, you yourself need to get your act together first. Never talk big and become a slave of your ego. Always be in a pursuit to improve yourself with each passing day.

Rule No. 7 is "Pursue what is meaningful not what is expedient." This is what I have been telling my Book Buddy community for the longest time. Instead of immediate and impulsive benefits in life, think long-term. Never cut corners because there is no shortcut in life. long-term success and accomplishments are achieved through perseverance, commitment, dedication and obsession. In today's era of instant gratification, people are reluctant to work hard over a long period of time and still expect favourable results. They might get some temporary fleeting success but nothing long-term can be achieved until and unless you don't pursue something meaningful for a long period of time.

Rule No. 8 is "Tell the truth or at least don't tell a lie." Almost every one of us is compelled to lie to impress others, to win arguments or to enhance our status. This fake attitude kills the life out of your life. No matter how hard-pressed you are, try not to lie.

Rule No. 9 is one of the best amongst the twelve rules and it goes like this: "Assume that the person you are listening to might know something you don't." When interacting with people make it a point to listen more and speak less. This will enable you to learn things which you don't know. I have often observed that when dealing with people we tend to be biased towards their outlook instead of the character that individual brings to the table. I have personally made the mistake of judging people on how they look physically; looks are really deceptive. In your communication, always look to learn from the person with whom you are speaking. This will open up new avenues of learning for you.

Never cut corners because there is no shortcut in life. Long-term success and accomplishment are achieved through perseverance, commitment, dedication, and obsession.

Rule No. 10 is very simple: "Be precise in your speech." First weigh, then speak. Your words are your identity and can make or break your game in no time. Therefore, be very careful with your language.

Rule No. 11 is the one due to which Dr. Peterson is controversial and famous as well. It goes like this: "Do not bother children when they are skateboarding." Superficially, this statement seems to mean that let children have fun without impeding their growth and learning. But it has an even more profound meaning. Dr. Peterson wants to say that today's modern society desires gender equality which means equal opportunity and rights for both males and females. However, biological differences can never be ignored. Equality of opportunity is a good thing but equality of output is a futile and ridiculous concept. He believes that there are major differences between males and females and they can never be equal. For instance, males have interest in things but females have interest in people. Similarly, males are disobedient but females are more agreeable. Our society follows a hierarchy and people who are competent move ahead regardless of their gender.

Equality of opportunity is a good thing but equality of output is a futile and ridiculous concept. He believes that there are major differences between males and females and they can never be equal.

Rule No. 12 is "Pet a cat when you encounter one

on the street." This rule personifies the main theme and central idea of the book. According to Dr. Peterson, suffering and grief are integral parts of human life. Every individual has a choice to either spend his whole life complaining or have the courage to create his future and establish a happy life. Enjoy the little things in life to maintain your balance and equilibrium.

Dr. Peterson is an international superstar because of his controversial and profound ideas. No matter how controversial they are, in my view he is an absolute thought-leader. Do give these rules careful thought and see which ones can make a positive impact in your life.

PERSONAL NOTES

Use this space to write your notes and key takeaways from the book.

PERSONAL NOTES

Use this space to write your notes and key takeaways from the book.

WINNING WITHOUT FIGHTING IS BEST

THE ART OF WAR
Author: Sun Tzu
Genre: Political Philosophy

The Art of War is a cult classic that was written around 2500 years ago by a Chinese General Sun Tzu. Even after thousands of years, its teachings are still relevant today; that is the reason why the world's top military, business, economic and political leaders read this book. Not only this, but it is also taught in leading military and business schools globally because it has got incomparable pearls of wisdom. If you are in a leadership position or aspire to be a leader one day, then read the next few paragraphs with great attention.

Due to its famous and mystical content, it has been translated into hundreds of languages. I still remember the time when my brother recommended me this book for the first time and remarked it as one of the finest reads ever, due to its path-breaking and unique concept. Its rhythmic and mystical style of writing makes it a read of a lifetime. It has got such a poetic charm to it that one is left mesmerised.

Its rhythmic and mystical style of writing makes it a read of a lifetime. It has got such a poetic charm to it that one is left mesmerised.

Superficially, the Art of War might seem like a book about war strategy but that is not true. According to the essence of this book, war is everything that brings difficulties in your life. Art of war is the name of fighting these difficulties and hurdles you might face during the course of your life. Thankfully, Sun Tzu has given us a plan. Let's see what it is.

Sun Tzu writes "Know your enemy and know yourself and in 100 battles you will never be in peril." What a meaningful statement this is, applicable to every aspect of our life. It means that in order to win, it is indispensable to be self-aware and have

complete knowledge of the opponent as well. This one principle will make you triumphant in almost all the battles that you undertake. Self-awareness is the key to success since it aligns you with your strengths and weaknesses which in turn helps you choose your battles wisely. Similarly, if you have a profound understanding of your counterpart or your opponent, you will be able to adjust your strategy accordingly.

Self-awareness is the key to success since it aligns you with your strengths and weaknesses which in turn helps you choose your battles wisely.

"When able to attack we must seem unable, when using our forces, we must seem inactive, when we are near, we must make the enemy believe we are far away, when far away we must make him believe we are near." All warfare is based on deception. This means that your success lies in deceiving your enemy. If your enemy understands your thought process and predicts your next move then you are gone. In this connection, Sun Tzu writes another breathtaking point in this book which states, "Let your plans be dark and impenetrable as night, and when you move, fall like a thunderbolt." The bottom line is that you need to keep on surprising your enemies in order to stay relevant in the game. All your moves should be calculated yet unpredictable. A pragmatic example of this point is the Pakistan Air Force retaliation to Indian aggression on 27th February 2019. On February 26, the Indian warplanes had entered Pakistani territory and dropped some bombs near Balakot resulting in nothing more than a few trees being destroyed. However, the news spread like wildfire, and the Indian media started lauding this as a great victory.

The Pakistani nation started looking at the army in the hope to fight back. India's entire military was fully ready for a counter-attack. However, Pakistan Air Force used the same tactics as prescribed by Sun Tzu. The whole day and whole night passed nothing happened. The next day in broad daylight, Pakistan Air Force attacked when the Indian military was least

expecting any sort of ambush. During the dogfight, Indian fighter pilot Abhinandan was captured and the rest as they say is history. The point is, warfare is the name of deception. In fact, not only war, even in your personal lives keep your moves calculated and covert.

One of my most favourite learnings from this book is "Winning without fighting is best." This comes across as a strange statement since the entire book is about war and its associated tactics. Basically, Sun Tzu strongly believes in the sharpness of the human mind, intelligence and his actions. He believes that a person's mind should be so razor-sharp that he should know what will happen even before the fight starts. Through negotiations, diplomacy, lobbying, research and analysis one should look to defeat his enemy instead of an on-ground fight. This is because war causes collateral damage in terms of human life and capital which depletes the resources of a state. Hence, it is best to avoid war with your intellect, strategy and diplomacy.

Through negotiations, diplomacy, lobbying, research and analysis one should look to defeat his enemy instead of an on-ground fight.

The next point is also very remarkable and it goes like this: "Military tactics are like unto water, for water in its natural course runs away from high places and moves downwards. So, in war, the way is to avoid what is strong and to strike what is weak. He who can modify his tactics in relation to his opponent and thereby succeed in winning may be called a heaven-born captain." A good leader is one who can attune his strategy according to the circumstances and conditions of his enemy. He is prudent enough to only engage with those who are weaker than him and avoid those who are stronger than him in terms of might and strength.

A good leader is one who can attune his strategy according to the circumstances and conditions of his enemy.

Another masterpiece statement that he attributes to a war general is that "When the general is weak and without authority, when his orders are not clear and distinct, when there are no fixed duties assigned to

officers; the ranks are formed in a haphazard manner that results in utter disorganisation." When a leader works without authority there will be no clarity in his command, he will be confused, won't be able to delegate work, will fail to nurture and grow people, hence there will be chaos and disturbance. Therefore, for any leader, it is very important that they have clarity of thought and supreme team management skills.

Sun Tzu was a master tactician who knew very well about the importance of foot soldiers in an army. Therefore, he wrote, "Regard your soldiers as your children and they will follow you in the deepest of valleys, look upon them as your beloved sons and they will stand by you even unto death." If you treat your team as your children, they will be willing to lay down their lives for you. There is a great lesson in this for those managers who are constantly bombarding the team and do not engage with them by using kindness and love as emotion. If you take care of your people, then they will go to any length to get you through.

The Art of War is brimming with these sorts of remarkable learnings which introduce you to new wavelengths of thinking. There is something new to learn in each paragraph which if understood and applied can elevate your personality and embark you on the journey to success in each "war" of life.

PERSONAL NOTES

Use this space to write your notes and key takeaways from the book.

SCALING
UP A BUSINESS
REQUIRES
OUTRAGEOUS
ENTREPRENEURIAL
ATTITUDE

MASTERS OF SCALE
Author: Reid Hoffman, Deron Triff & June Cohen
Genre: Business Management

A guru is an individual who has a thorough understanding of the ways of the world. He has wisdom, experience, intellect and a profound understanding of his discipline. A few gurus act as mentors as well to guide, coach and support you in every matter of life. I truly believe that in the tough journey of life one should have a guru who can guide you through thick and thin. You may find many experts around you who are competent in different disciplines however, it is hard to find a mentor who can give quality entrepreneurial guidance so you can go on to establish a successful business enterprise. Don't worry, because the leading entrepreneurs and masters of business have come together to coach you in a book titled "Masters of Scale" written by Reid Hoffman.

Reid Hoffman is a successful entrepreneur who has set up many companies over the years with the most notable being LinkedIn. On the internet, he runs his podcast with the title "Masters of Scale." In this podcast, he converses with top visionary founders and leaders from the business world who share their winning strategy with the public. He has compiled more than 100 of his interviews in the form of this book. Masters of Scale is filled with insights, wisdom and strategies that will inspire you to reimagine how you do business. It is indispensable for all of you, specially people who are studying commerce or pursuing a degree in business or aspire to be entrepreneurs, to learn from this book because it has the power to transform your lives. Some of the key points that Hoffman mentions are as follows:

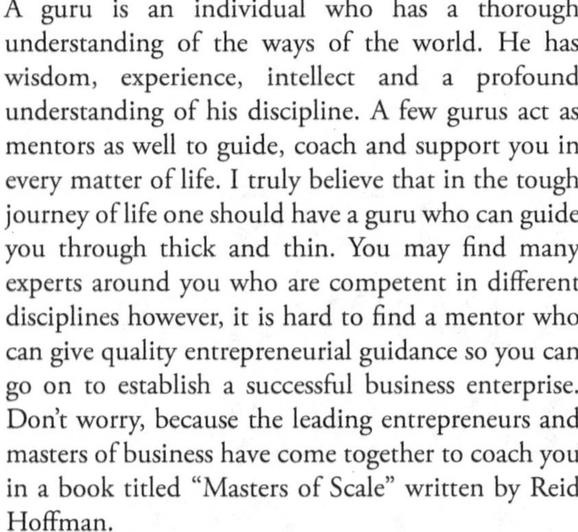

Masters of Scale is filled with insights, wisdom and strategies that will inspire you to reimagine how you do business.

1. How to handle NO
2. How to scale up a business
3. How to set company culture
4. How to grow fast
5. How to learn to unlearn
6. How to move to new business lines

Apart from this, there are umpteen examples mentioned in this book which will give you priceless learning. Let's discuss a few key points. Reid Hoffman refers to big businesses and claims that every big idea is contrarian i.e. it always goes against the norm. Whenever you discuss that idea with any person or investor, you receive a resounding NO. For instance, before the turn of the century, people used to find it ridiculous to make money from online searches through advertising but Google came and conquered it. Similarly, a few years back we could not have imagined that we would be commuting with a stranger in an unknown car who will give us pick and drop via a mobile app. However, today Uber has become a part of our lives. Similarly, no one could have imagined that every home had the potential of being transformed into a hotel where people could come, pay and stay; Airbnb has made it possible. Therefore, when people write off your business idea or say NO, see this as a sign that you are onto something big.

Another big concept that Hoffman alludes to is pertaining to customer delight. He states that giving a 5-star experience to your customers is a thing of the past. Successful companies today aspire to give an 11-star experience to their clients so they are glued to their services. In order to give an impeccable experience to the customers, you have to personally connect your product/service with the customer. When it comes to customer experience shoot for the moon because it will eventually be the catalyst which will enable you to scale up your business. Let me give you an amazing example regarding customer

experience, satisfaction and delight.

Nordstrom is a very famous store in the US where you can find footwear, apparel and clothes. One day a very angry person comes to a Nordstrom store and aggressively asks the team at the store to return snow tyres. Nordstrom and snow tyres have absolutely no connection. It turned out that Nordstrom's store had opened at the same site where previously there was a tyre shop and the individual mistook it for the store from which he had bought his tyres. He spoke angrily and insisted the Nordstrom team at the store immediately return his tyres and refund the amount. You won't believe what the manager did. He listened intently, calmed him down, kept his tyres and gave him a refund. Isn't this absolutely amazing? These acts make brands immortal and today even after so many decades this example is quoted in almost every business school to teach the concept of customer service.

Another critical thing that gurus of the business world practice is creating time and space every day to think about new ideas. Spanx founder Sara Blakely thinks about new ideas during her commute to the office even if she has to drive her car aimlessly on the roads. Caterina Fake, co-founder of Flicker's routine is to hunt for ideas between 2 am to 5 am at night. Reed Hastings, the founder of Netflix, hunts for ideas sitting in his living room. The purpose is to keep the brain active and on the hunt to put new ideas into practice.

There is a statement that is very famous in corporate circles and that is "Culture eats strategy for breakfast." This means that you can create the most high-powered and well-designed strategies but if your company's culture is stale, passionless and toxic then no strategy will ever work. Now the question is What is culture? It is basically a combination of many elements like:

- Employee Empathy
- Behaviour of Leaders
- Hierarchy of Structure
- Support Towards Initiative
- Communication
- Investment in Employees
- Power Structures
- Employee Boss Relationship
- Opportunities to Grow
- Company values

Top entrepreneurs state that the culture of the company should evolve with time and should be flexible. One thing is very important here i.e. your early hires will set your company culture. If you hire A-Graders, the culture will be A-Grade. If you onboard laggards then the culture will also be the same. It is therefore recommended to hire "learn it all" instead of "know it all" employees who continue to learn and evolve with time.

One thing is very important here i.e. your early hires will set your company culture. If you hire A-Graders the culture will be A-Grade.

When I teach business courses to my students, I always make it a point to let them in on the science of the S-curve. Whenever you launch any product, it will initially go from the early stage to the growth stage and eventually reach the maturity stage. At this stage, if you want to sustain the product or grow the business then the existing feature set will not be sufficient. Therefore, you have to invest in some new product or the existing product needs to be improved incrementally or exponentially. This cycle keeps repeating every few years when the products or business hits a plateau. This is called "pivot." Successful entrepreneurs are experts in pivoting from one product/business line to another to keep themselves relevant. This is why you will see significant changes in modern technology products every other month because they know that if they don't change, they will soon become irrelevant.

Successful entrepreneurs are experts in pivoting from one product/business line to another to keep themselves relevant.

The last point that I want to discuss pertaining to this

book is the concept of "Purpose before profit." This is one of the major differences between a businessman and an entrepreneur. When an entrepreneur starts a business venture his focus is not on making quick money. Instead, he is obsessed with offering a solution to a problem, contributing to society and creating employment opportunities. On the other hand, a businessman will always look at the bottom line. For entrepreneurs purpose supersedes profit. They are adventurers who are in love with their product. These sorts of individuals go on to become Jeff Bezos, Steve Jobs and Elon Musk.

For entrepreneurs purpose supersedes profit. They are adventurers who are in love with their product.

Masters of Scale is all about priceless suggestions and business recommendations from the top entrepreneurs of the world. One piece of advice can actually transform your life so always associate with people who can guide you in the best possible way. Analyse the people around you and ask yourself this question: Are you surrounded by quality people who have the potential to make you grow and be successful? If the answer is yes, then go ahead and make full use of them and if the answer is no then you need to seriously rework your associations.

PERSONAL NOTES

Use this space to write your notes and key takeaways from the book.

PERSONAL NOTES

Use this space to write your notes and key takeaways from the book.

51 BILLION TONNES TO ZERO CARBON EMISSIONS

HOW TO AVOID A CLIMATE DISASTER
Author: Bill Gates
Genre: Current Affairs/Politics

Bill Gates is one of the richest and most famous personalities on the planet and the co-founder of Microsoft. In the year 2015, he predicted a disease like Coronavirus which he said had the potential to kill millions of people across the globe. Lo and behold, the same virus disrupted the world in 2020 and turned our lives upside down. His prediction had come true. Bill Gates is an absolute genius who can peep into the future by understanding the pattern of things.

In the year 2021, he published a path-breaking book titled "How to Avoid a Climate Disaster." Basically, the premise of this book is that the climate across the globe is changing dramatically due to excessive global warming. Due to this phenomenon, many cities across the globe will be submerged underwater in the next 50 to 100 years. Not only this, but if we don't change the way we live our lives, there will be droughts, food shortages, rising temperatures and people dying of heat.

Bill Gates has profoundly alluded to all the perils climate change might bring in. The great thing about this book is that it gives a practical framework to all the countries and organisations that are making efforts to avoid a climate disaster. This book is my personal recommendation to all the individuals who are in positions of power and who want to play their part in saving the world from an impending climate catastrophe.

The book revolves around only two numbers; one is 51 Billion and the other is Zero. 51 Billion tonnes

are those greenhouse gasses that the whole world adds into the air every year. Greenhouse gasses (carbon dioxide, methane, nitrous oxide) are the gasses that trap the sun's heat into the atmosphere due to which the intensity of heat increases. He uses the number 0 because he aspires to have a net-zero impact of these gasses on our atmosphere. It's an almost impossible task to bring carbon emissions down to zero since everything from electricity to cement production, cars to plastic bags, ACs to microwave ovens, fertilisers to poultry farms emit these gasses. A fascinating thing is that even cows' belching and flatulence contains a massive amount of greenhouse gasses.

A fascinating thing is that even cows' belching and flatulence contain a massive amount of greenhouse gasses.

Now the question is how do we deal with this situation? It is the forte of Bill Gates that not only does he have the potential to identify the problem but he also proposes a practical step-by-step solution for the issue as well. Let's first have a look at our activities at which contribute towards the emission of these harmful gasses.

How much greenhouse gas is emitted by the things we do?

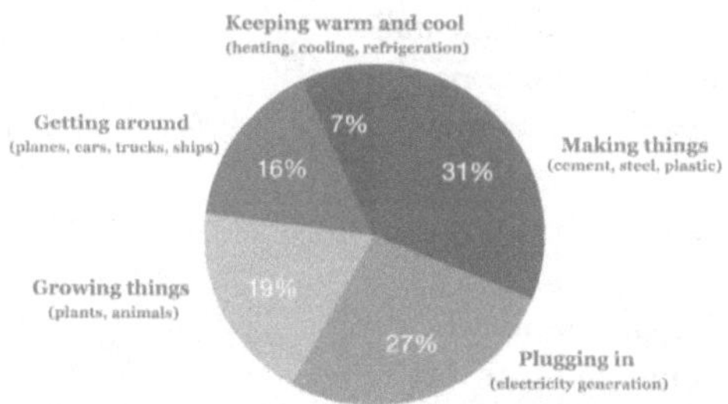

The table above suggests that most of the greenhouse gasses are emitted in cement, steel and plastic production which is 31%. After that comes electricity which is 27 % since most of the electricity is generated by burning fossil fuels. After that comes "how we grow things" which include plants and animals that are at 19%. At number 4 is "getting around" which means emissions due to all modes of transportation. Lastly, it's "keeping warm and cool" which is associated with managing temperature inside our houses and other facilities. The bottom line is that almost everything we do in our lives results in these harmful emissions. Now let's see how we can reduce them.

Firstly, Bill Gates believes that the grave issue of climate can only be resolved if governments across the world unite and work together to avoid future catastrophes that might arise. He also admits to the fact that clean energy is an expensive and capital-intensive task. He refers to it as Green Premium. This means that if you are paying Rs.18/unit to consume regular electricity, then it will cost Rs.25/unit to consume electricity that has been produced without burning greenhouse gasses. This gap between the two needs to be subsidized by the government through R&D and investment. He proposes that governments all over the world need to work on three fronts: Technology, Policy and Markets. Through the use of technology, innovative products should be made that help in reducing carbon emissions. In addition, renewable energy sources such as hydro, wind and solar, should be further improved. Through policy, the government should subsidise these products so that a common man can easily access them and through market development, their demand and supply should be aptly managed.

He also sets a few targets in the book where by the year 2050 the world should produce net-zero carbon emissions. On an individual level, he states that we should spread awareness in society about the detrimental effects of global warming. We should also change the way we consume energy. For example, replacing regular house bulbs with LEDs, controlling our carbon footprint and making efficient use of energy. He also suggests that people should shift their demand towards electric cars so our dependence on fossil fuels can be reduced.

Now the point comes that whether or not a country like Pakistan will benefit from buying electric cars where 90% population cannot afford a motorbike. This is one of the prime reasons why people from the developing world do not pay heed to the discussion about climate change, greenhouse gasses, carbon emissions and global warming. We are perennially stuck in the vicious circle of making ends meet; why would we care about the rise in temperatures?

However, even for developing countries, it is pertinent to know what the future holds. This book is a complete white paper, a manual for those countries who want to work on greenhouse gasses, carbon emissions and reduction of global warming.

Apart from providing a roadmap for avoiding a climate disaster, this book stands out due to the genius of Bill Gates. It is a breathtaking testament to his problem-solving skills where he breaks down an issue into several parts and solves them one by one. His mind is very logical, clear and solution-oriented, something we should all aspire to possess.

Apart from providing a roadmap for avoiding a climate disaster, this book stands out due to the genius of Bill Gates.

PERSONAL NOTES

Use this space to write your notes and key takeaways from the book.

TECHNOLOGY IS OUTPACING HUMAN ADAPTATION

FUTURE IS FASTER THAN YOU THINK

Author: Peter Diamandis and Steven Kotler
Genre: Business Management

Technology has transformed our lives inside out. The world of computers, internet, social media, big data and artificial intelligence has taken our lives by storm. There was a time when we used to write letters to our loved ones and used to wait for days and weeks anticipating a reply. In today's world, we can use several communication applications to convey our message using voice and video chat within a matter of seconds. Almost all facets of our lives have been impacted by modern technology. The rate at which technological innovation is happening surpasses human adaptability by miles. What we used to consider as science fiction is finally becoming part of our reality. In this regard, a very interesting book has been written by Peter Diamandis and Steven Kotler titled "Future Is Faster Than You Think" which highlights how future technologies are overwhelming the world around us.

The authors of this book have tried to discuss that in today's modern world the secret behind technological growth and its breathtaking speed is "Convergence" which means a blend of two or more technologies. Whenever such convergence occurs, technology grows at an exponential speed and results in disruptive innovation. An example of this cutting-edge innovation is autonomous cars which can run without the driver behind the steering wheel. Experts say that in the next few years self-driving cars will be so pervasive that a special permit will be required to bring human-operated cars on the road.

Another benefit of these self-driving cars will be a significant reduction in road accidents. There are about 1.2 Million deaths due to accidents globally every year and ninety percent of these happen due to driver's fault. If there will be no drivers then there will probably be no accidents. This is because computers and algorithms by then would have become so smart and mature that there would be no room for error. As a result, our roads will be much safer.

If you keenly observe the above example, you will infer that two professions are becoming obsolete: drivers and car insurance companies. Technology not only creates new opportunities but its flip side is that it bulldozes whatever comes in its way.

Technology not only creates new opportunities but its flip side is that it bulldozes whatever comes in its way.

On the other hand, when it comes to travel and transport, Elon Musk aspires to make people travel anywhere in the world within an hour. He intends to use the same rocket that he will use to transport people to Mars. The name of this rocket is "Star Ship" and it travels at the speed of 17,500 miles/hour. It can make you travel from New York to Shanghai in 30 mins, London to Dubai in 29 mins and Hong Kong to Singapore in only 22 mins.

Your phones have already transformed into smart machines. In the future, you will just have to order your phone to execute a task and it will be done. For instance, your phone will be able to schedule your appointment with the barber or reserve your table in the restaurant by itself. This will be done through the use of Artificial Intelligence and Machine Learning. Let's take this example one step further. In the future, when you order pizza don't be surprised if your conversation with the pizza guy goes in the following direction:

Your phones have already transformed into smart machines. In the future, you will just have to order your phone to execute a task and it will be done.

Phone ringing
Operator: Good afternoon sir. Thanks for calling Galaxy Pizza.
Customer: I would like to order pizza.
Operator: Let me confirm your multi-purpose

number. It is 8614-554-60. Ok so, you are Mr. Shahrukh who is speaking from House No. 101, Precinct 31, Bahria Town. Karachi having house phone number "40942366" and your office phone number is "764523020" and your mobile phone number is "033312345678"

Customer: What! From where did you get all my phone numbers?

Operator: Sir we are connected to the central database.

Customer: Ok anyways, I would like to order seafood pizza.

Operator: It will not be good for your health sir.

Customer: How come?

Operator: According to your medical report, you have high blood pressure and your cholesterol level is also high.

Customer: What? So, what do you suggest me?

Operator: You can try our low-fat pizza. You will definitely like it.

Customer: How do you know?

Operator: Last week you borrowed a book from the national library titled "popular low-fat dishes."

Customer: Ok I give up, give me two family-size pizzas. How much will it cost?

Operator: There are a total of 7 people in your family so for them it's enough. Your total bill will be Rs. 6000

Customer: OK I can pay through my credit card, right?

Operator: I am so sorry sir you need to pay via cash. Your credit card limit has exceeded and since October last year, you have to pay Rs 1 lakh to the bank and that doesn't include late payment of your housing loan.

Customer: Ok let me get the money from ATM before your delivery man comes to my home.

Operator: Sir unfortunately, you cannot withdraw cash from ATM as well, since you have crossed your daily cash withdrawal limit.

Customer: Oh God, never mind, you please send me

the pizza. I'll get the cash ready. By the way how long will it take?

Operator: It will take about 45 minutes sir. If you are in a hurry, you can come on your own scooter.

Customer: What?

Operator: According to our information you have a "1969 vintage scooter" with registration number "USE 8999." Do you want to know anything else?

Customer: Nothing, I just want to know whether you are sending me three cola bottles with the deal?

Operator: Sir I would have definitely sent it but as per our record you are diabetic as well.

Customer: WTF@#$.

Operator: Sir, mind your language. On 11th Nov 2005 when you were driving your 1999 Honda civic with registration number AUG 4260 at that time due to traffic violation, you abused a police officer for which you had to pay a heavy fine.

Friends, don't laugh at this curiously outrageous situation. This is what you will see happening right in front of your own eyes and it will be possible due to two technologies. One is the "Internet of things" and the second is "Artificial Intelligence," Every device around us will carry sensors that will allow the devices to talk to each other and share information. For example, if there are not enough eggs in your fridge then you don't need to go to the bakery to fetch them, your fridge itself will order eggs. Similarly, if you are in your car and getting late for work then you don't need to tell anyone because your car will inform your office by itself.

Another important thing that technology will do is extend the lifespan of humans. Almost a hundred years ago the average lifespan of a person was thirty-five or thirty-six years. However, because of pharmaceuticals, antibiotics and use of clean water life span has increased to an average of sixty to sixty-five. In countries like Japan average age is 80+. In the next few years, you will frequently find people who

are aged 110 or 120 years and still living a healthy life. You will also be surprised to know that some companies are trying to cheat death like Google-owned Calico, Unity Biotechnology which Jeff Bezos is supporting, Alevian, Samumed and Cellularity.

Moreover, in the future, everyone will have his own personal AI digital assistant that will know you inside out even better than your own self. It will know about your mood swings and will adjust itself accordingly. It will look after your medical appointments, will take care of your health, will entertain you, and on your behalf will go to the market or do online shopping.

The way we educate our children will also transform. By the year 2030, if a student wants to go to school, he will wear his VR gear and lo and behold, he will be in his school. There he will decide himself what he has to study, the way he wants to study and the speed at which he wants to study. Every child will have his own teacher that will not be a human but an artificially intelligent machine, which will develop its students as powerful thinkers and empathetic individuals.

Doctors will no more be required for diagnostics and healthcare. All you have to do is wake up in the morning and ask your phone "How is my health?" and within seconds, it will give you a complete detailed report regarding your health, your heart rate, blood sugar level, vitamin level, temperature etc. It will tell you if you have a fever, will diagnose the virus and let you know about the place at which you became infected by it. It will also consult a robot doctor online regarding your sickness and within no time the medicine will be at your doorstep.

All of this is not science fiction but a soon-to-be reality. This is what the authors of this book have tried to communicate. All of these things might seem

outrageous to you, but the reality is that it is just a matter of time before all of this starts happening right in front of our eyes. Our aim should be to move ahead with time and learn modern technology so that we stay relevant in the larger scheme of things. I strongly urge you to teach yourself and your kids STEM (Science, Technology, Engineering & Mathematics) subjects so you can develop a thorough understanding of modern science and innovation. It will not only be beneficial for yourself but will also contribute a lot towards the upliftment of our country.

PERSONAL NOTES

Use this space to write your notes and key takeaways from the book.

AS THE
COMPANY
GROWS,
THE SIZE
OF ITS
FAILURES
SHOULD
ALSO GROW

INVENT AND WANDER
Author: Jeff Bezos
Genre: Business Management

Mark Zuckerberg, Elon Musk, Larry Page, Sergey Brin, Larry Ellison and Jeff Bezos are some of the most prominent entrepreneurs known across the globe. An entrepreneur is a person who flows against the tide to create something novel and new for the world. His prime purpose is not to make profits but to solve a societal problem. Entrepreneurs are never afraid of failure and feel very comfortable taking risks. They are passionate and obsessed to the point of insanity about their product. This is what differentiates an entrepreneur from a businessman. In the next few paragraphs, I will discuss one of the most successful entrepreneurs of the modern era and one of the richest men in the world, Jeff Bezos.

Jeff Bezos is one of those individuals who with his effort, intellect and smart business intelligence has changed the way we live our lives. Jeff Bezos started amazon.com in the year 1994, where he used to sell books online. Gradually, he developed amazon into an everything store and the biggest e-commerce platform in the world. In order for the general public to know more about his thought process, he has published a book titled "Invent and Wander" which is a compilation of Jeff's letters, press talks and interviews. This book carries colossal learning for its readers especially for aspiring entrepreneurs who want to make it big in the business world. Let's discuss what the great guy is all about.

Jeff Bezos was very clever and sharp since childhood. During his early years, he aspired to become a theoretical physicist but soon realised that he didn't possess the right aptitude for it. Therefore,

he completed his graduation in computer science and went to New York to pursue work. In the year 1993, he came across a statistic that shook him to the core which mentioned that the internet is growing at the rate of 2300% per year. This triggered an entrepreneurial storm in him and he started realising a big opportunity was on offer. He resigned from his job and started writing a business plan for his new company which he named Cadabra; this company went on to become amazon.com.

In the year 1993, he came across a statistic that shook him to the core which mentioned that the internet is growing at the rate of 2300% per year. This triggered an entrepreneurial storm in him and he started realising a big opportunity was on offer.

Amazon today is the largest e-commerce company on the planet. It employs more than 1 Million people across the globe. It started off by selling books online; when it gained considerable traction, they further introduced music and CDs as well. This portfolio continued to grow and now almost any item that you can think of is available there.

Besides e-commerce, Amazon has many different products that are very successful like Amazon web services which are considered as the best cloud computing products. Amazon Kindle is a very beautiful gadget that brings millions of books to your screen. Amazon app store from where you can access millions of apps. Amazon game studios which produces computer games and a new retailing concept where without paying cash you can shop and go. Apart from this, Jeff Bezos has another company called Blue Origin. This company is trying to make space exploration accessible and affordable for all.

This book helped me understand the qualities that Jeff possesses which have helped him to become so uber-successful. Let's discuss some of his personality attributes.

Bezos lives his life on an interesting principle known as the "Regret Minimization Framework." When making a big decision in life, he visualises that when he will be 80 years old and reminiscing this decision,

Bezos lives his life on an interesting principle known as the "Regret Minimization Framework." When making a big decision in life, he visualises that when he will be 80 years old and reminiscing this decision, will he regret it or not.

will he regret it or not? This thought process always enables him to make high-quality decisions that have high risk and high impact. Some of these decisions work and some don't but the secret behind his success is that he is never indecisive. He celebrates his successes and failures equally.

Another unique and interesting thing about Jeff Bezos that I came to know after reading this book is that he dislikes PowerPoint presentations. He states that Amazon doesn't have a PowerPoint culture. If any employee wants to give any input or idea then he can communicate via a six-page long memo. He believes that the narrative that can be conveyed through six-paged memos cannot be conveyed through a PowerPoint slide deck. This enables his people to be sharp, succinct and comprehensive when conveying their feedback and ideas.

Amazon doesn't have a PowerPoint culture. If any employee wants to give any input or idea then he can communicate via a 6-page long memo. He believes that the narrative that can be conveyed through 6-paged memos cannot be conveyed through a PowerPoint slide deck.

Another very interesting mantra that he lives his life on is "Day 1." It's been 27 years since Amazon has existed but the energy there is still like Day 1. In fact, the building where Jeff resides is named Day 1. He believes that as a company moves towards Day 2, first it becomes irrelevant and then obsolete. Therefore, specially at the leadership level, you need to maintain hustle and speed so employees always feel that it's Day 1. Another critical thing about Bezos is his high-velocity decision-making process. He never suffers from analysis paralysis and believes in quick decision-making. He also believes that if you have 70% knowledge of any issue, make an immediate decision. If you wait for 90% then you will miss the bus and eventually be late. When making a decision, use 70% data and information and the rest 30% base it on your gut feeling and intuition.

Another critical thing about Bezos is his high-velocity decision-making process. He never suffers from analysis paralysis and believes in quick decision-making.

Another aspect that stands out about Bezos is his unusual thought about failure. He believes that as a company grows, the size of its failure should also increase. Isn't this unusual? He says that if this doesn't

happen that means you are not innovating enough and you will naturally fall behind. He is never afraid of multi-million-dollar failures since he is aware that one successful product can cover ten failed products. Here, he also differentiates between experimental and operational failure. He is absolutely inflexible about operational failure and has no tolerance for it. However, if we are experimenting, trying to make something new and striving to go from zero to one then there is no shame in such a failure.

The most bizarre and wild thought of this man is pertaining to the future of planet Earth. He believes that in the coming years our planet will run out of resources due to a consistent increase in population. Therefore, we need to have a manufactured world somewhere in space which has got all facilities that our Earth possesses like transport network, homes, parks, agriculture, etc.

Whatever we enjoy in the world should exist over there as well. His greatness is that he knows that this will not happen in his life but he wants to play his part to lay the infrastructure for future generations. Isn't this such a great, future-driven and people-centric thought?

You must follow people like Jeff Bezos and learn from them. They might have their own set of personality weaknesses but in general, they are absolute thought leaders of the world. Pick up a diary and note down all the attributes which you like about his personality and make sure that you imbibe some of them.

PERSONAL NOTES

Use this space to write your notes and key takeaways from the book.

ALWAYS CARRY A BOOK WITH YOU

WHO WILL CRY WHEN YOU DIE

Author: Robin Sharma
Genre: Self-help

Who Will Cry When You Die? Have you ever given this question a thought? I personally think that it's a missed opportunity if you are not able to leave a legacy during your lifetime. Legacy is a word which means, "Did I matter?" It means to die but not to perish. If you live a meaningful and purpose-driven life that is driven by the desire to help the people and the community around you then surely you will leave a strong legacy behind you. This point has been made the center of gravity for this book titled "Who Will Cry When You Die" written by Robin Sharma. Robin Sharma is a stalwart in the discipline of self-help who has influenced the lives of millions of people across the globe through his powerful writing. This book further cements his place in the top self-help writers of all time. Let's discuss some key takeaways from the book.

In Who Will Cry When You Die, the author has mentioned 101 things that you can adopt and make part of your personality so that you leave a rich legacy behind you. I have selected five out of these 101 points that I find the most meaningful. Let's delve deep into them.

In Who Will Cry When You Die, the author has mentioned 101 things that you can adopt and make part of your personality so that you leave a rich legacy behind you.

The first point is starkly simple and that is "Get up early." This might seem very trivial but it can turn out to be the single biggest contributor to your success in life. People who wake up early can execute and perform more efficiently compared to late risers. In the morning, dopamine levels are at their highest which allows you to focus more and be more productive. If you observe the lives of people around you, you will realise that almost all successful people

have a habit of waking up early. Early mornings carry mercurial power which allows an individual to be more organised, methodical and disciplined. These factors eventually lead to enhanced productivity during the day. If regular workouts are made part of your early morning routine, then you simply become unstoppable. If you don't trust me then try it yourself. You will soon find out what a big blessing it is to rise early and start your day. Give yourself one hour of isolation early morning. During that one hour, you can exercise, meditate, read and learn something new. These activities compound over a period of time and give you colossally improved results.

The second point is "Take more risks." It is easier said than done but time and again it has been proven that individuals who have a penchant for taking risks end up living a much more fulfilling life. Risk is directly proportional to returns in life: higher the risk higher the return. If you are timid and live your life within the norms set by society then it is highly likely you will fall into the trap of mediocrity. Influential people always keep on pushing the envelope and take calculated risks to keep moving ahead in life.

The third point is my personal favourite, can you guess? It is "Always carry a book with you." Such a simple yet profound postulate propagated by Robin Sharma. An individual who falls in love with books and makes reading part and parcel of his/her lifestyle is bound to have elevated self-awareness and self-esteem. This is because reading gives them comprehensive knowledge about the world that we live in. It is a window into the beautiful world of knowledge and wisdom. The habit of reading is the most common habit amongst people who excel in life. Moreover, books allow you to meet with the leading stalwarts of their time like Aristotle, Plato, Socrates, Karl Marx, Sun Tzu, Machiavelli, Leo Tolstoy, Charles Dickens, William Shakespeare, Roald Dahl,

Jules Verne and the list is endless. Books help you develop your personality and a mature thinking mind which in turn attracts people towards you. Through the medium of books, I got the opportunity to connect with all wonderful people like you who are interacting daily with me through social media handles (currently I have 200,000 followers across social media). The sort of support, encouragement and unconditional love that you have given me has only been possible because of books.

The fourth point is the "Rule of 21." You might have heard this before as well. Basically, this rule alludes to the creation of new habits. It is famously believed that it takes 21 days to nurture a new habit. However, Robin Sharma negated this fact in his book The 5 AM Club where he extrapolated that it takes 66 days to install a new habit (you can read about this in my review of the The 5 AM Club in this book). I have always strongly believed that first you make habits and then habits make you. Therefore, make sure you cultivate the right set of habits because they will eventually collate to develop your personality and make you successful.

The last point that I want to discuss is a bit controversial and unique and that is "Be an Impostor" which means pretend what you are not. This might seem counterintuitive since in popular culture we are always taught to be genuine and honest. What Robin Sharma is trying to suggest here is that you need to change colours according to the situation you are in. Life is mostly driven by circumstances that are mostly out of your control. Therefore, in order to live up to the expectations of people you need to ensure that you are attuned to your environment. For instance, if you are an introvert but your job requires you to be an extrovert then there is no harm in faking it. In fact, this is a quality that you need to imbibe in your personality so that you can face every tough situation with ease and are not overwhelmed. Being

an impostor also helps you in being flexible in life and being a learn it all instead of being a know it all.

The bottom line of the book is that you have to make your life meaningful and purpose-driven. I believe that the greatest meaning you can give to your life is by dividing it into two halves. In the first part of your life invest in yourself, read, learn, progress and reach the state of self-actualization.

Once you touch the peak you have decided for yourself, start giving everything back to the community by disseminating your wisdom, learnings, experience, fortune, wealth and your time. This will help you in being influential and leaving a strong legacy behind you.

PERSONAL NOTES

Use this space to write your notes and key takeaways from the book.

EMBRACE YOUR WEIRDNESS

HOW TO BE INTERESTING
Author: Jessica Hagy
Genre: Self-help

It is the desire of almost every individual to possess a charismatic and attractive personality so that people would want to become associated with him. If you think you don't have a charming personality and your presence is not so magnetic then don't worry because in the next few paragraphs, I will tell you principles which if followed well will enhance your aura by manifolds and you will become the talk of the town.

The first thing that you need to do to make yourself interesting is to "suppress your fears of life." Society wants to drive every individual in a particular way, do not fall for this trap. Try to untangle and unplug yourself from the norms and break free. Explore yourself, expose yourself and come out of your comfort zone. Keep inquiring and asking questions no matter how embarrassing it is for you. Always be on the lookout for facts which are opinions and opinions which are facts. Slowly and gradually your brain will begin to unravel and you will have new avenues of thought.

> *Society wants to drive every individual in a particular way, do not fall for this trap. Try to untangle and unplug yourself from the norms and break free. Explore yourself, expose yourself and come out of your comfort zone.*

The second thing is to "share what you discover." Any novel thing that you discover in life, make sure you share it with people. It will give you a tremendous feeling of joy (this is the same joy I experience when I post videos for all of you). An idea shared is not diminished, it's multiplied. As is popularly said that knowledge is a treasure that grows as you disseminate it. Expand your circle of acquaintances for this will enable you to meet people from all walks of life which will give you new experiences, new discoveries and new learnings.

> *An idea shared is not diminished, it's multiplied.*

The third step is to "do something, anything." Never sit idle and be content with it. I always say one thing to all of you that no great deed can ever be accomplished without consistent long-term struggle. Fuel the curiosity inside you and keep moving ahead. I still remember the statement written by Einstein in a letter he wrote to his son: "Life is like riding a bicycle; in order to maintain balance, you need to keep moving."

Fourth is to "embrace your weirdness." There are some unique traits in every person's personality that separate one person from another. Appreciate and acknowledge these idiosyncrasies of your personality since they will help you stand out from the crowd.

Fifth is to "have a cause." There must be a purpose and a passion behind your existence. If your life is purpose-driven it will be a meaningful life. Living a rudderless life that is sans any purpose is a missed opportunity. There should be some obsession and passion that should constantly be driving you forward.

Sixth is to "minimise the swagger." Control your ego and your arrogance since people don't like arrogant people at all. If you observe the vast and infinite universe, you will realise that the presence of an individual is absolutely trivial and insignificant. Don't forget this. Try to focus on the things which you don't know and always be a lifelong student. Learn different skills across the span of your life. If you commit mistakes in the way of your pursuit towards gaining more knowledge, let them happen. After all, you are a human and not a robot.

Seventh is to "give it a shot." Remember, action cures fear in life. If we wait for things to happen, they never will. You have to take control of the steering wheel of your life. Individuals who are driven by destiny and fate never end up doing something meaningful

in their life since they surrender to metaphysical concepts. Your success is not driven by amulets or lucky charms rather it is your consistent hard work that contributes towards your success in life. Dream big and have the capacity to follow those dreams as well so you can transform them into reality. There is no shame in thinking big and having big goals; whatever your mind can conceive it can achieve.

Eight is to "hop off the bandwagon." Avoid becoming part of the crowd since it will make you lose your identity. Carve your own path, so that instead of you being the follower, people start following you. If you observe people, you will see that majority of them conform to the established standards and norms set by society and end up living a mediocre life. What's happening around you and has been followed since centuries does not necessarily have to be true. Always question things and develop something new.

Ninth is to "grow a pair." The less fear you have, the better your quality of life will be. If you think the wavelength of your thought process is different, make it known to the people around you. You will be amazed at how many people will join you. Comfort, safety and ease are the swamps of your life that trap you without your even noticing. Be stubborn and use it positively. You might create a mess on the way to your destination but that is ok. The end will justify the means.

The tenth step is to "ignore the scolds." There are three circles in life: one is "could have", second is "would have" and third is "should have" and at the intersection of these three comes "didn't do anything". This simply means that instead of

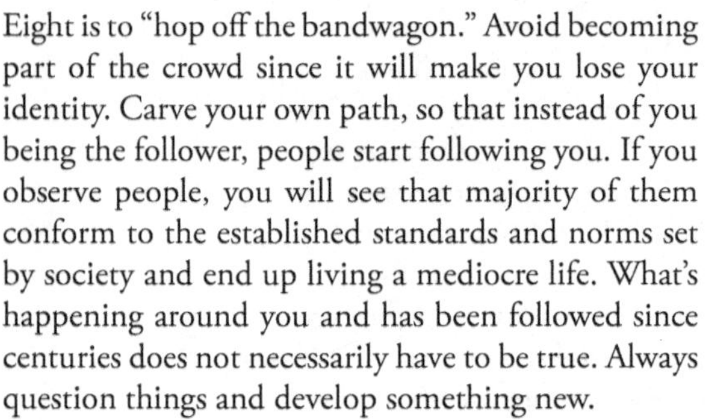

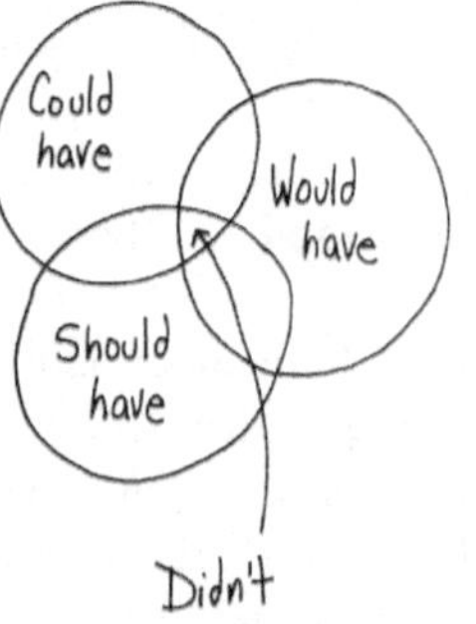

just aspiring for things, you need to act and make it count. Merely talking about things and giving lip service won't do you any good. If you have to grow and be a source of inspiration for the people around you then just do it.

This is as far as this book is concerned. If you want to know my point of view, the only thing that can make your personality interesting is your go-getter approach and the ability to offer something new to people every time they meet you. If you are a laggard and a big-time procrastinator, people will never get attracted to you. Being energetic, lively and respectful towards all will in turn make you attract the right people in your life since they will find you inspirational and interesting.

PERSONAL NOTES

Use this space to write your notes and key takeaways from the book.

THE SECRET TO A LONG AND HEALTHY LIFE IS TO LIVE A PURPOSE DRIVEN LIFE

IKIGAI
Author: Francesc Miralles and Hector Garcia
Genre: Self-help

There is an island in Japan named Okinawa. The special thing about this island is that it has the highest number of centenarians in the world (people who have reached the age of 100 years). The people living here have the longest life span in the world. You will find dozens of people who are living a healthy and prosperous life even after crossing the 100-year mark. Researchers over the years have tried to find the reason behind their longevity of life. A few of them suggest that their diet is very simple and healthy and they use a lot of green tea which keeps their system clean. A few conclude that the climate of that area is what makes them live so long. A few researchers also attributed their long life to the clean water available to them. Upon a deeper dive, it was revealed that there is something more powerful that helps them live longer than anyone else in the world and that is "Ikigai." It is the magic of Ikigai that the people of Okinawa are not only the oldest people in the world but also live strong, healthy and very happy lives. This concept has been remarkably explained in the book titled "Ikigai." Let's get to know what it actually is since it can also help you live a long, healthy, and meaningful life.

Ikigai is a Japanese word that means to live a meaningful life. People of Okinawa recognize their Ikigai very early in life. They are always engaged in work in which they find maximum happiness. This is a concept similar to logotherapy (I discussed this in my review of Man's Search for Meaning). Their work becomes dovetailed to their purpose in life and that is what wakes them up with joy in the morning. It's a simple yet very profound concept that states

that in order to live a happy life you need to have a life driven by purpose. This requires finding out the things in life which you are good at, something in which you can excel and then weaving your life around it. However, there is a catch to this. There might be many things in life you are good at but they might not necessarily contribute towards your happiness. Therefore, not only do you need to find something you are good at but that same thing should also be a catalyst towards you achieving happiness in life. This is demonstrated by the following diagram.

There might be many things in life you are good at but they might not necessarily contribute towards your happiness. Therefore, not only do you need to find something you are good at but that same thing should also be a catalyst towards you achieving happiness in life.

The above diagram is a combination of four circles. The first circle is "what you are good at" followed by "what you love" then "what the world needs" and finally "what you can be paid for." These four circles blend your passion with profession, mission and vocation. If you carefully construct your life around these four circles you will lead the most prosperous life ever. This concept will help you understand why most of us are unhappy in life. This is because mostly we try to do work which we are good at, which the world wants as well and we can get paid for. However, the most important element of loving what you do is missing. We spend all our lives in pursuit of money by doing something we don't like which eventually

leads to sadness, anxiety and perennial despondence. Realisation of this core concept of life is what makes this book a worthy read.

There are several other things mentioned in the book which can help us transform our lives. For example, the people of Okinawa do not have any concept of retirement. These people keep on working as long as their health allows regardless of what age they are at. This helps them stay dynamic and busy which keeps them going for long periods of time.

The people of Okinawa do not have any concept of retirement. These people keep on working as long as their health allows regardless of what age they are at.

"Hara Hachi Hu"- you might have never heard this statement but this expression is an integral part of their life. Japanese people repeat this phrase before and after every meal. This is a reminder that while eating you should only fill up your stomach up to 80%. This helps them avoid overeating and doesn't tire their digestive system too much. If you have been to Japan or you have eaten at a Japanese restaurant, you might have noticed that they serve food in four to five small plates. This helps them create an illusion that a person has eaten sufficiently which helps them balance the calories due to which they remain fit and strong.

The third big reason for the long life of the people of Okinawa is that they do not take excessive stress. You might have observed people around you who, due to living a stressful life, age prematurely. Stress is the leading cause of premature aging. Research by the American Institute of Stress has shown that most illnesses are caused by stress which in turn affects your skin, heart and digestive system. In today's lightning-paced world, it is almost impossible to keep yourself calm and composed, since we are constantly bombarded by innumerable stimuli during the day. We are living our lives in a state of emergency and constant alertness which negatively impacts our overall well-being. However, it is quite amusing that while a lot of stress plays a negative role in a person's life, low level of stress in fact contributes towards the growth of an individual. Howard Friedman, professor at the University of California, Los Angeles, has discovered that people who manage stress and carry a little bit of it throughout their life eventually end up living a very long, healthy and successful life.

Two major causes of premature aging are sitting on the seat all the time and not getting enough sleep. After the invention of computers, the trend of working from one stationary seat throughout the day has become a norm. While this has contributed to the overall progress of humanity, it has had a tremendously negative impact on the health of people.

Sitting across the day leads to the occurence of diseases like hypertension, osteoporosis, obesity and cancer. When you do not do physical activities or exercise, there is a cell in your immune system called Telomere which starts to deteriorate. This causes your cells to grow old leading you to old age eventually. This book also enlightens us on the tips to stay young, hale and hearty.

Sitting across the day leads to the advent of diseases like hypertension, osteoporosis, obesity and cancer.

Ensure that you go on a walk for 20-25 minutes on a regular basis. In your daily routine, whenever you get a chance, try to climb stairs instead of using the lift. Replace fast food with seasonal fruits. Identify all such activities which are not good for your health and throw them out of your life and make sure you get the right amount of sleep (I have spoken at length about the importance of sleep in my review of Why We Sleep).

Ensure that you go for a walk for 20-25 minutes on regular basis. In your daily routine whenever you get a chance, try to climb stairs instead of using the lift. Replace fast food with seasonal fruits.

Let's discuss the diet of the people of Okinawa as well. Bradley Wilcox and Makoto Suzuki have specially written a book on their diet with the title "The Okinawa Program." They discovered that in total they eat around 206 types of natural food.

In a single day, they eat 5 to 6 different types of fruits and vegetables. They also eat a lot of grains and consume very little sugar and salt. On average they eat only 7 grams of salt in a day while the rest of the Japanese people consume around 12 grams a day. Their calories consumption is 1785 calories/day while people, in general, eat 2068 calories/day. They also consume healthy food like tuna, carrots, goya, onion, sweet potato, soya bean and cabbage which helps them in staying young.

Ikigai is surely a remarkable book that enlightens your soul. I urge all of you to take note of what you have just read and try to imbibe the habits of the people of Okinawa in your life. You might end up becoming a Centenarian.

PERSONAL NOTES

Use this space to write your notes and key takeaways from the book.

PERSONAL NOTES

Use this space to write your notes and key takeaways from the book.

KARACHI WAS ONCE KNOWN AS PARIS OF THE EAST

KARACHI – ORDERED DISORDER & THE STRUGGLE FOR THE CITY

Author: Laurent Gayer
Genre: Politics/Current Affairs

A stalwart of Urdu poetry, Parveen Shakir, wrote the most appropriate thing about Karachi. She said, "Karachi is like a prostitute to which people of all wallet sizes from mountains, plains and deserts come and spend a night with. Not only do they fulfill their sexual desires during the night but in the morning give a tight slap on its face and then leave for work in anticipation of the coming night." Over the years I have heard so many things about Karachi but none has been so ruthlessly honest. Today, when I look at the innumerable social issues of Karachi pertaining to infrastructure and human development, I feel Parveen Shakir was right to a tee.

Karachi holds the key to the overall success of Pakistan. It is the financial hub of the country and the biggest metropolitan we have. It houses people from all walks of life and provides them with employment opportunities. However, we haven't done justice to the city at all. In the year 2022, it should have been on par with the likes of Dubai, Bangkok, Istanbul and Singapore but it is not a part of this elite league. The history of Karachi and its struggle was beautifully covered in the book titled "Karachi-Ordered Disorder and the Struggle for the City" by Laurent Gayer. It discusses the pre and post partition history of Karachi, student union conflicts, Sindhi Muhajir dissension, Altaf Hussain and MQM, Lyari peace committee and other pertinent issues which have been monumental in shaping up the history of Karachi. Let's discuss them briefly.

Karachi holds the key to the overall success of Pakistan. It is the financial hub of the country and the biggest metropolitan we have.

Karachi back in the day was a fisherman's settlement named Dirbo. Dirbo is derived from an Arabic word

Karachi back in the day was a fisherman's settlement named Dirbo. Dirbo is derived from an Arabic word "dirb" which means entry. This was known to the Arabs as the gate of Hind.

"dirb" which means entry. This was known to the Arabs as the gate of Hind. Modern Karachi was established by a few Hindu traders after a nearby port Karak Bandar became dysfunctional due to excessive sand and mud. This prompted them to create a new port which was named Dirbo which eventually went on to become Karachi. Another very interesting thing that I learnt from this book was that during World War II, American soldiers stationed in Karachi were given a booklet called "Guide to Karachi." In the guide, it was mentioned that Karachi is Paris of the East and the cleanest city in the whole of India. Keeping in mind the sorry state of affairs of today's Karachi, this statement seems quite unbelievable.

This book carries some really remarkable statistics as well. For instance, when the census of Karachi was done in 1941, 51% people of Karachi were Hindus and 42% were Muslims. This shows that the Hindu community had a big role to play in the early development of the city. After partition when the census was conducted in 1951, 96% of the population was Muslim and only 2% was Hindu. This, in a way, is very sad since a society based on pluralism thrives more due to inclusivity. This is the reason why we have white colour in our flag which denotes our respect for people belonging to other religions and promotion of inter-religious harmony. Hindus and Parsis were the most educated, forward-looking and progressive communities of Karachi. The contribution of the Hindu community is further illustrated by the fact that from 1911 to 1921 the President of KMC was Seth Harchandrai Vishandas, who was a Hindu. He is referred to as the father of modern Karachi due to his unmatched execution of development for Karachi, specially its infrastructure. He made a lot of modern roads like Mcleod Road which we today call Ibrahim Ismail Chundrigar Road or I. I. Chundrigar, Elphinstone road which is called Fatima Jinnah Road now and M.A Jinnah Road which is known as Bander Road as well.

This book also speaks in detail about the importance of Karachi University in the overall politics of the city. Laurent Gayer has remarkably explained how the University of Karachi was established, how Jamiat used to rule there, how Altaf Hussain established APMSO in 1978 which later became MQM, how these groups fought each other and eventually had a significant impact on the overall political landscape of the city.

No story of Karachi can be complete without mentioning the name of Altaf Hussain. A detailed explanation has been given about his personality, his political movement, his party creation, party discipline and how he created a cult-like following. It also sheds light on the ethnic conflicts of the city which horrified its residents for thirty years starting from the incident of Bushra Zaidi in the year 1985.

One thing which made me sad about the whole situation was that when the author finishes this book in 2014, he paints a gloomy picture of Karachi. He predicts more ethnic violence, security issues and infrastructure disaster. The ray of light is that when I write this review in 2022 the security situation has remarkably improved in the city. There are no more daylight murders that were customary in the city of Karachi. Since 2015, after Rangers took action, the situation is under control due to which the economy of the whole city has really improved.

We need to understand the geostrategic location of Karachi as well as Pakistan. Global population is around 8 Billion out of which approximately 3 Billion people are living very near to us as neighbours in countries like China, India, Bangladesh, Afghanistan and Iran. This means that Pakistan, especially Karachi, is situated at the crossroads of rising powers. It could be a leading pathway that connects Central Asia with Europe. However, it is lagging behind in terms of what it can aspire to be.

Therefore, it is my request to the stakeholders of this city whether it's Sindh or Federal Government, to do something meaningful for the people of Karachi. I want to further request the citizens of Karachi to take the ownership of the city in their hands. We are the direct and most important stakeholders of the city. We should consider it as our motherland, as our city, as our home. Until and unless we do not contribute at the individual level towards the overall upliftment of the city, we will never be able to see our city prosperous and progressive. Let's prove Parveen Shakir wrong.

PERSONAL NOTES

Use this space to write your notes and key takeaways from the book.

I WANT TO COLONISE MARS

ELON MUSK
Author: Ashlee Vance
Genre: Business

As I am writing this text, Elon Musk is currently the richest man in the world. For the people who are not aware of this gentleman, I just want to say one thing: If someone asks me today "Who is the most valuable man on the planet?" It will be Elon Musk. His stature has nothing to do with his bank balance, wealth or fortune. In fact, what makes him such a sought-after individual is his vision for humanity. His personality attributes are so inspiring that every human should learn from him. That is the reason why I made it a point that he will surely be a part of my first book. His biography has been written by Ashlee Vance titled "Elon Musk – Tesla, Space X and the Quest for a Fantastic Future." The book gives vivid insights into the personality of this great man. Let's delve into it.

As I write this, the current net worth of Elon Musk is $195 Billion. You can imagine the extent of his fortune by keeping in mind that the total GDP of Pakistan which has over 220 Million people is around $280 Billion. This means that one person's fortune is equivalent to almost 70% of our total economy. If Elon Musk were a country, he would have been the 50th richest country in the world. He wasn't this rich from the start but made his way forward by creating the most cutting-edge and innovative companies during the course of his career.

Today he leads several entrepreneurial ventures which are considered to be market leaders in terms of their products and services. He is the founder and CEO of Space X, a company that has revolutionised space travel and will be the first one to take people

to Mars. He is also the CEO of Tesla, a company that is a pioneer in making the most breathtakingly innovative electric cars. Due to Elon Musk's vision and hard work, Tesla last year became the most valuable motor car company in the world. Next is The Boring Company, another venture which Elon Musk leads as a founder. This company is looking to revolutionize the daily commute of people by offering under-ground travel service, hence reducing the traffic congestion on the roads. Another venture of Musk is Neuralink which is connecting human brains to artificial intelligence.

The story of Elon Musk starts in South Africa where he was born. During childhood, one trait which made him stand out was his voracious reading habit. He used to be so engrossed in reading that his mother used to think he has turned deaf; since whenever she used to call him, he never responded. He used to read one book after the other without any break. This habit eventually led to the development of his cognitive and intellectual capabilities. He credits his reading habit to whatever he knows today specially about space sciences although he doesn't have a formal degree in it.

He credits his reading habit to whatever he knows today specially about space sciences although he doesn't have a formal degree in it.

Eventually, he migrated to the USA and went on to set up one of the most successful companies in the business world: PayPal. He was one of the founding members and made PayPal an absolute success story. After selling PayPal off, whatever money he got he invested into the two most future-driven companies which no one could have thought of at that time, Space X and Tesla.

Through Space X, Elon Musk intends to change the face of space travel. He found space travel very expensive and decided to revolutionise it by introducing reusable rockets for the first time. This single innovation reduces the cost of space travel significantly. Another aspiration that Musk has with

Space X is that he wants to make humans a multi-planetary species by colonising Mars. He wants people to travel between Earth and Mars as easily as they travel between two countries. For a common man, this might seem very bizarre and impossible but for a mercurial and genius mind like Elon Musk, this is very much achievable. In fact, he has given himself a personal target of the year 2025 for hundreds of people to be living on Mars.

Another aspiration that Musk has with Space X is that he wants to make humans beings a multi-planetary species by colonising Mars. He wants people to travel between Earth and Mars as easily as they travel between two countries.

Another interesting thing about this great man's personality is that he thinks life is very short. Therefore, he wants to achieve things quickly. He gives himself tight deadlines and is triumphant most of the time. He has a theory behind completing things that is simple yet very hard to accomplish. He says that on average people work for 45 to 50 hours a week. If I simply double this time by working for 90 to 100 hours per week, I will be able to accomplish things way quicker than the rest of the world. This is the reason why he is very ruthless about his work habits where he works for 16 to 18 hours a day. There are often times when he has to sleep on the floor of his Tesla factory to ensure that he stays on top of things.

He is very ruthless about his work habits where he works for 16 to 18 hours a day. There are often times when he has to sleep on the floor of his Tesla factory to ensure that he stays on top of things.

There are many takeaways from this book, especially about Elon Musk's personality. One thing which I have personally learnt from Musk and imbibed in my personality is persistence and perseverance. For the longest time, Elon Musk couldn't see light at the end of the tunnel for Space X. He was burning cash every day but none of his rockets were successful and most of them blew off. He spent years and years perfecting Space X and developing a rocket that is efficient as well as cost-effective. After 5 years of establishing Space X, when he was on the brink of a nervous breakdown and Space X on the brink of bankruptcy, he finally became successful. Since that time onwards, there has been no looking back. He has made Space X super successful through his long-

term commitment to the cause.

Another habit of his that strikes me the most is his reading habit. Despite being one of the busiest people, he makes sure that he spends time reading books. This helps him in staying updated and creating new neural pathways of learning which eventually help him to achieve more and break down complex problems into reliable solutions.

One fascinating thing about Elon Musk is that he is an Expert Generalist. He has master-level expertise in different fields whether it be Space Sciences, Artificial Intelligence, Automation, Renewable Energy or Design. He has a curious and imaginative mind which works in various directions. He is a classic case of a human being utilizing his optimum genetic potential. This one attribute of his personality attracts me the most since it gives me the inspiration to work harder and discover new avenues of thinking.

I have loved to read biographies and autobiographies of successful people since childhood. It allows me to peek into their lives and circumstances. Moreover, I get to learn a lot about their positive and negative qualities. I urge you to do the same and read about people who have contributed in making this world a better place. This will enable you to adopt their positive habits and will give you a reference point to take key decisions of your life. It is always great to have a mentor who has achieved substantially in his life. I, through this book, want to wish the great Elon Musk all the best for his ventures.

PERSONAL NOTES

Use this space to write your notes and key takeaways from the book.

LIFE CARRIES A MEANING IF THERE IS AN INHERENT STRUGGLE ATTACHED TO IT

EVERYTHING IS F*CKED
Author: Mark Manson
Genre: Self-help

Mark Manson became an international best-selling author because of his book "The Subtle Art of Not Giving A F*ck." The unusual concept of this book made him a superstar in the reading community around the globe. He has written his third book as a follow up of the same book which is titled "Everything is F*cked." It's easily Mark Manson's best book because its concept is very unique, unusual and profound. Mark, through his books, has introduced a new genre in the world of self-help books known as pessimistic self-help. Every book claiming to be self-help has more or less similar things mentioned in it like "Yes, you can do it, whatever your mind can conceive it can achieve, the law of attraction works without fail, think big, think positive, focus in life" etc.

Mark through his books has introduced a new genre in the world of self-help books known as pessimistic self-help.

Mark Manson, on the other hand, doesn't mince his words and calls a spade a spade. He very rightly believes that life is a name of struggle and there are ups and downs in every person's life. There is nothing like an ideal fantasy world. You have to explore your way through the hardships of life through a meaningful struggle that intrinsically carries a feeling of joy. A happy life is one that is laced with an inherent perennial struggle in pursuit of a worthy ideal. This is the main theme behind this book as well.

A happy life is one that is laced with an inherent perennial struggle in pursuit of a worthy ideal.

He starts off by talking about the progress paradox which is quite a unique and counterintuitive idea. It states that materially this is the best time to live in human history. The world is progressing at the speed of light and almost everything that a person

can think of is available to him. However, as humanity continues to progress; the pain, suffering, depression, despondence and anxiety of people also continues to increase. In today's world, we have thousands of choices at the click of a button. Having so many options should make our lives easier but it never happens. Information overload has made us less informed and more irrational. People of the modern age suffer from serious mental health issues despite being so well off.

Mark Manson explains the reason for this despondence which is quite similar to the one the great mathematician and scholar Bertrand Russell gave in his magnum opus "The Conquest of Happiness" (I have reviewed that book as well). Most of the people are living a hopeless and sad life due to the absence of struggle in their life. Remember, if there is no struggle, meaning or purpose behind your existence you will never be happy. I have observed that majority of the people live a rudderless life without any meaningful goals. There are a few people who set goals but they are so trivial that they are easily achieved leading to further cluelessness.

When you remove the friction from your goals and desires, they become meaningless. As long as there is a passion, obsession, restlessness and relentlessness associated with your life you will always be happy. Living well doesn't mean the absence of suffering but it means suffering for the right reasons.

Mark Manson believes that the opposite of happiness is not sadness rather hopelessness. Despair is the greatest enemy of our happiness. A pessimistic person who has no hope in life can never be happy. You will hear a lot of people saying that do not expect or be hopeful about anything from any individual. Since these sorts of people live their life without any hope therefore, they rarely live a happy life. There is a term for this condition in psychology known as "Anhedonia" which means the loss of ability to experience joy even on the most joyous of occasions. Now the obvious question is, "Why are people hopeless in life?" According to the author of this book, there are three main reasons. First is a Sense of Control, second is Belief in Something and the third is Community. If these three things are solid then your hope will remain intact and you will be able to sustain it for a long time. When all three or any one of these things are weak, you will be frustrated and hopeless.

Out of these three, Sense of Control is pivotal to sustaining hope in life. However, Mark Manson believes that sense of control is an illusion. To understand this concept, he gives an analogy of a consciousness car. This car has two passengers, one is the thinking brain and the other is the feeling brain. The thinking brain feels it's in charge since it knows about the crossroads of life and can decide prudently when to turn left and when to turn right. However, it is actually the feeling brain that is present on the steering wheel and takes the final decision on matters of life. It will do whatever it wants, often times shunning away all the reasoning and logic. The art of taking things in your hand is to make your feeling brain understand the importance of rational thinking so that it can opt for the best for you in every situation.

One of the best things that stands out for me in this book is the most remarkable example of maturity and adulthood that Mark Manson has given. He writes that a child is immature because he wants what he wants without having any inhibitions. He can sit in a Chinese restaurant and ask for a *roti* or be stubborn about drinking a cold drink despite having a sore throat. A person becomes mature when he can put a barrier between himself and his desires. A mature individual knows that if he wants to achieve anything, he needs to have solid hard

A person becomes mature when he can put a barrier between himself and his desires. A mature individual knows that if he wants to achieve anything, he needs to have solid hard work and struggle behind it.

work and struggle behind it. He develops the ability to step into painful situations and sacrifice instant gratification for long-term happiness. Mark Manson believes that in today's world there is a depressed level of maturity. Everyone wants instant gratification and instant fame due to which they abhor struggle, hard work and perseverance. He states that there can be no stability in our world unless there is maturity across the human race. There is a dire need for us to place higher principles and values before anything else.

You know friends, when I was reading this book, I felt very happy and intrigued. This is because what Mark Manson has written was known to me at least ten years back. It's not that I am pompous about this, it's just that due to excessive reading and exploration I was able to untangle the deep secrets of life. When a person is on the move and pragmatic, he is always able to get the answers to his existential questions. Therefore, I urge you to keep exploring and most importantly keep asking the right questions because your pursuit will eventually lead you to exploring happiness. Remember, life is like riding a bicycle; in order to maintain balance you need to keep moving.

When a person is on the move and pragmatic, he is always able to get the answers to his existential questions. Therefore, I urge you to keep on exploring and most importantly keep asking the right questions because your pursuit will eventually lead you to exploring happiness in life.

PERSONAL NOTES

Use this space to write your notes and key takeaways from the book.

276

GOOD
RESULTS IN LIFE
ARE DIRECTLY
PROPORTIONAL
TO FOCUS

THE POWER OF FOCUS
Author: Mark Victor Hansen
Genre: Self-help

In today's technology-driven world where we are bombarded with innumerable stimuli throughout the day, it is very hard to maintain focus in life. While the advent of social media has been a great source of advantage for humanity, it has had a disastrous impact on our attention span. Attention span means how long we can concentrate on any one thing. Most people can't focus on one thing for more than a few seconds. One major culprit in our disintegrated attention span is social media whose unlimited scrolling has ruined our minds. We want to experience a dopamine rush every few minutes in the form of new notifications and triggers which leads to perpetual distraction throughout the day.

Laser sharp focus is one of the key ingredients of success. Your focus is what will get you through in life and set you apart from the crowd. Therefore, I want to talk about how you can actually maintain and sustain focus as I dissect the book "The Power of Focus." In this book, the author has mentioned 11 strategies that you can follow to restore focus in your life. I will discuss a few of the best ones in the next few paragraphs.

Let's start with a very potent one, "Your habits will determine your future." Remember, first you make habits and then your habits make you. The higher the quality of your habits, the higher the quality of your life. One of the best ways to develop good habits is to identify those around you who are successful. Observe them very keenly and then gradually imbibe their winning habits in your personality. Once winning habits are developed your focus will be

automatically taken care of since you will be attuned to live your life according to a schedule.

Next is "Focus on the things you do the best." In order to be productive, you need to play to your strengths so things happen effortlessly. Identify your areas of brilliance and start working on them. List down three things that you are really good at and gradually make them part of your life. Learn to say "no" to things that you are not good at executing.

In order to be productive, you need to play to your strengths so things happen effortlessly. Identify your areas of brilliance and start working on them.

Next comes "Do you see the big picture." This means defining your goals and making sure they are meaningful. You need to make sure that your goals are yours and not borrowed from here and there. There must be logical reasoning behind what you want to achieve. Ask yourself what will be the rewards and benefits once you achieve them. You also have to ensure that your goals are specific and measurable. For example, instead of just stating that I want to lose weight or I want to be financially independent or I want to migrate to a foreign country you can state that "I want to exercise 30 minutes a day four times a week" or "I want to earn 5 Million Rupees in the next 5 years" or "By 2023 I want to settle in a European country." These statements are measurable, specific and realistic.

You also have to ensure that you are not fixated and inflexible about your goals. There are always several ways of doing things. Moreover, your goals must be in alignment with your personal values like honesty, integrity, faithfulness, kindness, etc. They should intrinsically carry a weightage of contribution to society. This will not only make you super focused but will also give you the ultimate delight in life.

Your goals must be in alignment with your personal values like honesty, integrity, faithfulness, kindness.

Another strategy is the "Confidence Factor." In the absence of confidence, fear and worry grip you and keep you distracted. If you are not confident then your chances of being distracted multiply. Many

people inquire from me the steps needed to build confidence, I would recommend the following six:

- Every day remind yourself that you have done something well.
- Read inspiring biographies and autobiographies. This is my favourite since it helps me get inspired by people who have made it big in the world.
- Be thankful. No matter how bad your circumstances might be. There is probably someone worse off than you, so always be grateful.
- Build excellent support around you. People who are with you unconditionally.
- Push yourself to accomplish short-term goals. This will provide the necessary fuel to keep the fire inside you burning.
- Try to attain financial independence in life as soon as possible. Nothing can boost an individual's confidence more than financial liberty and security.

Another one is "Consistent Persistence." What a remarkable point and one of my favorites. I always advocate the fact that perseverance is second to none when it comes to personality traits. The more consistent you are, the more you will excel in life. I have spoken in detail about this concept in my review of "The Compound Effect."

I always advocate the fact that perseverance is second to none when it comes to personality traits. The more consistent you are, the more you will excel in life.

Another strategy to improve your focus is to take decisive action. Don't overthink and get trapped in an analysis paralysis. Once you decide something, just do it. Most people spend their entire lives procrastinating due to which they never execute things. Procrastination is one of the biggest reasons behind losing focus in life. There are primarily four reasons why people procrastinate.

1. They are bored. This boredom doesn't make them feel enthusiastic about anything in life.

2. They are overwhelmed with work. They have so much work that it piles up as time passes and within no time they don't know where to start.
3. They are doing work that they do not enjoy at all.
4. They are easily distracted or downright lazy.

Lastly, one of the best strategies to improve your focus is to live a purpose-driven life. If your life is purposeless then it's a hopeless life.

In case, you have failed to find purpose in life so far then don't worry, keep moving ahead because eventually your action will cure your fear and lead you to a much more focused and fulfilling life. Remember, the fewer distractions you have in your surroundings, the better you will be able to focus, and focus is directly proportional to good results in life.

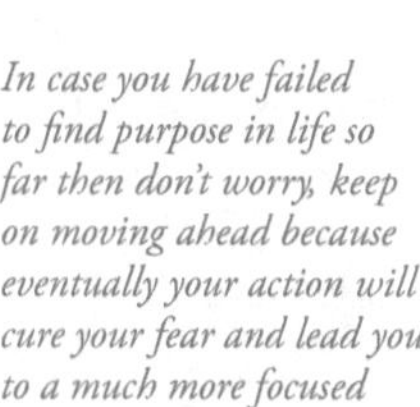

PERSONAL NOTES

Use this space to write your notes and key takeaways from the book.

BUSINESS IS DONE WITH PASSION AND OBSESSION, KEEP GOING EVEN IN THE TOUGHEST OF CIRCUMSTANCES

SHOE DOG
Author: Phil Knight
Genre: Business/Biography

There are a few modern entrepreneurs who stand head and shoulders above the rest due to their unique approach to business. Phil Knight, the founder of Nike, is one of them. He has made Nike an absolute powerhouse in sportswear. Today, the word Nike is tantamount to the most premium quality of sports clothing, footwear and accessories. His philosophy behind running a business is what has made Nike what it is today. Right from its inception, Phil Knight was driven by the desire to contribute rather than just make profits. He always intended to make life better for people through his products which is the reason why even in the toughest of circumstances he persisted in his efforts. He has let the world know about the history of Nike and his personal struggles through his memoir "Shoe Dog". It is the most fascinating book which covers the entire journey of Nike from a very small shoe store to a global giant. Moreover, it helps you peek inside the mind of its great founder so you know how he made the company so big. Let's discuss what Shoe Dog is all about.

Shoe Dog was published in the year 2016 and became an instant hit due to the motivational story and unique writing style of Phil Knight. It is not a quintessential business book rather a very profound and philosophical account of how he and Nike made it big. He has been vividly honest in the book and has openly accepted his mistakes so that young entrepreneurs learn from him.

Shoe Dog was published in the year 2016 and became an instant hit due to the motivational story and unique writing style of Phil Knight.

The book takes us in the year 1962 when Phil Knight was a young 24-year-old boy. He had been at the

University of Oregon, Stanford Business School and subsequently spent a year in the US army. He always wanted to be an athlete but due to his limited talent, he couldn't excel in it. However, he wanted to be associated with sports in any way possible.

The book takes us in the year 1962 when Phil Knight was a young 24-year-old boy. He had been at the University of Oregon, Stanford Business School and subsequently spent a year in the US army.

While he was studying at Stanford, he had come across a research paper which stated that Japanese running shoes will one day overtake American running shoes and become dominant. This thought jolted him and being the go-getter that he was he immediately convinced his reluctant father to sponsor his trip to Japan to understand what was actually going on there. In Japan, he met the team of Onitsuka Company, who were, the makers of Tiger athletic shoes. Knight shammed to be a representative of a US shoe importer, "Blue Ribbon" and arranged for samples to be sent back home to the US.

Knight juggled between his work at an accountancy firm and spending his spare time selling Tiger shoes. Very soon he had sold out his first shipment and ordered another 900 after taking a loan from the bank. In the year 1966, Knight's first employee, Jeff Johnson, opened Blue Ribbon's first retail store, in Santa Monica. The business continued to grow and sales kept doubling every year but Knight always had liquidity issues due to which he had to face a tough time with the banks as they kept declining his credit line.

This was the time when Onitsuka was actively looking for a new US distributor to replace Blue Ribbon. Knight kept working on his brand and eventually developed it as Nike with its ubiquitous and famous swoosh logo. Nike, as a brand was first introduced to the world at the National Sporting Goods Association Show in 1972. The shoes picked up and Nike started getting big orders. Onitsuka got to know that a new shoe brand with the name Nike was coming head-on in competition with them.

Nike, as a brand was first introduced to the world at the National Sporting Goods Association Show in 1972.

They cut off the supply and decided to sue Nike for going against the agreed terms and conditions.

This was the time when Phil Knight showed his leadership skills and stood in front of his people to tell them that there is an opportunity in every adversity. This was the time to create their own shoes instead of acting as mere resellers for a Japanese brand. The team worked together and developed the Nike brand in leaps and bounds. Knight, along with his partner Bowerman, continued to experiment with the running shoes to make them better in design and performance. With each passing year, Nike became the favourite of American runners who liked its modern design. The Cortez was the first running shoe to take pressure off the Achilles tendon, which made it the best choice for leading runners in the country.

While Nike continued to grow, its problems and issues also started multiplying with the banks and courts. Finally, it won its case against Onitsuka and was free to pursue its journey independently. 1976 Montreal Olympics proved to be a game-changer for the brand as leading athletes were wearing Nike shoes letting the world know of its worth. This was the time that Phil Knight thought of going public and finally made it in the year 1980. After eighteen years of struggle Knight was finally successful in listing his company at the New York Stock Exchange.

Phil Knight continued to run Nike as CEO for forty long years before hanging his boots in the year 2007. During those forty years, he had made Nike the leading brand with sales of $16 Billion, the year he retired. The book gives a very profound account of how to deal with failure and adversity. It also shows how conviction and dedication can help people and companies grow. One of the best things that Knight advises people in this book is "don't stop." It is very easy to give up in the toughest of circumstances

but it takes positive personality traits like courage and valour to keep marching ahead. Once I read this book, I was bursting with motivation. It gave me a new understanding of dealing with tough circumstances and staying steadfast. That is the reason why I always encourage my followers to read biographies and autobiographies since they give first-hand information into the lives of people who have made it big. Shoe Dog and Phil Knight are truly inspirational.

PERSONAL NOTES

Use this space to write your notes and key takeaways from the book.

ONE IS NOT BORN A WOMAN, BUT BECOMES ONE

THE SECOND SEX
Author: Simone De Beauvoir
Genre: Philosophy

I have always told you that the majority of what is published or what we read is run-of-the-mill literature. However, there are a few books that pass the test of time due to their sublime content and become part of superior literature. They not only influence individuals on a personal level but can inspire global movements as well. "The Second Sex" written by the remarkable French philosopher Simone De Beauvoir falls in this category. It is a masterpiece and one of the finest pieces of philosophy ever written. Its content is so raw, profound and ruthlessly honest that it is subject to a lot of controversies as well. No one has propagated the philosophy of feminism in the way Simone did. Her unique and peculiar style of thinking when it came to women is what sets her apart. She has personified her unique thought into this book. Let me dissect this masterpiece for all of you.

The central idea of this book revolves around the following statement, "One is not born a woman but becomes one." This one statement lays the foundation stone for the entire feminist movement. Therefore, you need to understand this well. What Simone is trying to communicate revolves around the philosophy of "Existentialism" which states that "Existence Precedes Essence." This means that your existence dominates everything else and determines how you will live your life. When someone is born, instead of being labelled with a particular gender, they should be allowed to pursue and find their essence themselves. Therefore, when a girl is born, she is not a woman- she is made a woman by her society, her civilisation, her history, her culture, her experiences,

"

her parents, her siblings and her relatives who force her to live her life according to the established framework of the society. This framework makes a woman dependent on men for her existence, forces her to forego her identity and live her life under the strong pressure of patriarchal forces.

Simone de Beauvoir used to hate this idea and starts the book with the question, "What is a woman?" She states that throughout history man is considered as default while women are treated as a secondary gender or the "Other." She says that humanity is always considered as male and female instead of being seen as herself or in singularity; is always defined relative to the male. This is the reason why she named this book "The Second Sex." She further builds up her case by writing that a women have been exploited and suppressed by men since ancient times. According to her, male dominated society at large tends to think that a woman has merely just two responsibilities, one is to have children of these men and the other is to provide them sexual gratification, that's it.

She states that throughout history man is considered as default while women are treated as a secondary gender or the "Other."

Historically and culturally, this is the only purpose of women all over the world and men have deliberately conditioned them into it. This has been done by not allowing them to leave the house, disarming them from learning any skill, suppressing their desire to acquire knowledge and develop a thoughtful mind.

This conditioning has led to the complete dependence of woman on man who keeps her trapped in a vicious domestic circle throughout her life. This was the reason why she openly disclosed her hatred for housewives who she believed did not carry any economic value. Their existence or non-existence is equal. Housewives, she believed were an insult to humanity since they are fully dependent on a man who whenever he wants can drive them out of his home and marry another woman. This was the reason

Housewives, she believed were an insult to humanity, especially women, since they are fully dependent on a man who, whenever he wants, can drive them out of his home and marry another woman.

why she was against pregnancy as well and believed that having children is a curse that holds women back. If you look at her personal life, she never got married due to her highly polarised views towards males. Although she had a life-long affair with Jean-Paul Sartre, a famous French philosopher, yet they never married. She has also made it very clear in this book that having children is the ultimate right of the woman. If she doesn't want children, it is perfectly fine. No one should ever force her into getting pregnant and having children. She abhors the thought that the majority of women, instead of carving their own identity, choose to spend their life through their children, giving up on their dreams, desires and aspirations.

She has also made it very clear in this book that having children is the ultimate right of the woman. If she doesn't want children, it is perfectly fine. No one should ever force her into getting pregnant and having children.

There are several other bizarre ideas that she has propagated in this book. For instance, she says that the way a mother breastfeeds her boy is different from the way she feeds her daughter. Therefore, the discrimination starts from the woman's womb. As girls grow up, they are overtly and subliminally conditioned to behave in a particular way and discriminated against. When a boy is growing up and shows signs of naughtiness, it is considered tantamount to being clever and sharp and he is encouraged and supported while if a girl is naughty or stubborn, she is rebuked. From childhood, she is made into a woman, a woman who is repressed and economically dependent on men.

She gives an outrageous analogy of a doll to support her argument. Since childhood, a doll is considered to be a girl's best friend. People don't realise, but there is subliminally a toxic conditioning going on in the back of her mind. Dolls symbolise perfection: fair skin, long thick hair, beautiful dress, big round eyes, toned body and perfect make-up. This is the kind of image that girls grow up idealising and internalising. When they are growing up it becomes indispensable for them to look as alike as possible to a doll.

This thought in turn disturbs their psychological equilibrium and pushes them to behave in a particular way. This ideal image objectifies women; which is actually what men want. Women do not groom themselves to look beautiful or pretty rather deep inside they want to somehow be acceptable to a man. Simone De Beauvoir takes her outrageous thoughts a step ahead and blames "a mother" for all this. Since she is the one who trains her daughter to behave in a particular way that is acceptable to men.

As is evident, Simone strongly opposes patriarchy. A patriarchal system is one in which males hold ultimate authority and power. She absolutely dismisses and ridicules it to the core. She prompts women to not succumb to this system and motivates them to look at themselves with a new pair of eyes instead of looking at themselves from the eyes of men. She wants women to be independent and carve an identity for themselves which is based on freedom and liberty in which they are free to make their own life decisions.

In her conclusion, Beauvoir looks forward to a better and brighter future for women where there is equality of opportunity, equal pay and equal rights. This book is the most profound and appropriate elaboration of the concept of feminism. I personally do not agree with her opinions on marriage, children and housewives. However, she makes perfect sense when it comes to women being given equal opportunities without any sort of discrimination. I have always taught you to view things objectively without bias and prejudice. Whether you agree with Simone De Beauvoir or not, one thing cannot be denied; The Second Sex is a remarkable piece of literature that should be read by everyone.

PERSONAL NOTES

Use this space to write your notes and key takeaways from the book.

I HAVE
ALWAYS
DREAMT
BIG AND
THIS
HAS GIVEN
ME THE
GREATEST
ADVANTAGE

THE ART OF THE DEAL
Author: Donald Trump & Tony Schwartz
Genre: Business/Biography

Who doesn't know Donald Trump? He is one of the most outrageous men in the world. Even before becoming the President of the USA, he had a cult fan following due to his success as an entrepreneur and television appearances which catapulted him to global fame. Donald Trump invites the most polarised reactions across the globe. People who love him, love him to the core while people who hate him do it with full voracity. Love him or hate him, Donald Trump is a phenomenon who has made it big through his sharp and shrewd mind. He is dangerously ambitious and due to his aggressive winning attitude he has seen a lot of success and prosperity in his life. He has disseminated his wisdom and experience through a 1987 book titled "The Art of The Deal" which gives an insight into his interesting and peculiar personality. It gives the reader meaningful information on how to make it big in the business world by using the power of mind, personality and negotiation. Since we as a nation are obsessed with real estate, therefore, it is a great learning for people who want to deal in buying and selling land. Let's get to know what it is all about.

Trump talks about his father, Fred, who was a successful developer of rent-controlled housing in the New York boroughs. Young Trump learnt the art of business very early in life when he used to accompany his father on construction sites. In college, while his friends were carelessly reading comics and going through sports pages, he was rigorously going through listings of property foreclosures. He always had big dreams of erecting landmark projects in Manhattan, the most premium

place for real estate in the world. Since childhood, he had a penchant for dreaming big which gave him a great advantage over his contemporaries. Whatever he had thought of in his life, he ended up achieving due to his positive mindset.

Here he drops a tip for all the people dealing in real estate. He states that it's a myth that location is everything in real estate. What people need to do is to create an aura, a mystique around the property that will persuade the people to buy it, regardless of its location. He promotes big talk and the use of words like spectacular, biggest, greatest. No wonder he uses a lot of this hyperbole in his speech as well.

He states that it's a myth that location is everything in real estate. What people need to do is to create an aura, a mystique around the property that will persuade the people to buy it, regardless of its location.

The book gives a deep insight into the strengths of his personality. Superficially, he might come across as very flashy and arrogant but one of the biggest qualities that Donald Trump has in his repertoire is patience capital. He has the attitude to wait for things and then pounce as soon as an opportunity arises. He discreetly states that stubborn perseverance is the ultimate difference between success and failure.

Superficially, he might come across as very flashy and arrogant but one of the biggest qualities that Donald Trump has in his repertoire is patience capital. He has the attitude to wait for things and then pounce as soon as an opportunity arises.

Here again, he drops a tip: he exclaims that while making a deal the worst thing you can possibly do is seem desperate to make it. Control your emotions and try to probe what the seller needs or wants and give them something extra in addition to your offering.

While making a deal the worst thing you can possibly do is seem desperate to make it. Control your emotions and try to probe what the seller needs or wants and give them something extra in addition to your offering.

One of the secrets of Trump's success is his inbuilt instinct of handling complex matters. He thrives during challenging times. He personifies the statement "there is opportunity in every adversity." What might seem like a dead-end to most of the people, for Trump it is the foundation of a new start. He has proved it time and again in his career as a successful entrepreneur. He states that to be successful in business one must balance boldness with patience and caution.

Trump credits his love for glamour to his mother and his rigorous work habits to his father. He is an individual with a big heart who is very strict on principles. Though he is famous for his line "You are fired" courtesy his TV show "The Apprentice" but in reality, he hardly lets anyone leave his company. He himself exclaims that "In my life, there are two things I've found I'm very good at, overcoming obstacles and motivating good people to do their best work." He is often portrayed by the media as arrogant and outrageous, someone who is big in his boots but in reality, he is an individual with a very strong self-belief. He believes in fighting his way through the calamities of life no matter how colossal they are.

He is often portrayed by the media as arrogant and outrageous, someone who is big in his boots but in reality, he is an individual with a very strong self-belief.

Towards the end of the book, he presents his softer or rather philosophical side. He asks himself a question, "What is the meaning of all this wealth, fortune, and empire?" and gives a starkly honest answer that he doesn't know, but he derives fun in doing whatever he does. The Art of the Deal might not be the best book on profound business learnings but it provides some priceless takeaways on the art of doing business along with offering a window into the mind of a great man.

PERSONAL NOTES

Use this space to write your notes and key takeaways from the book.

PERSONAL NOTES

Use this space to write your notes and key takeaways from the book.

DISRUPTIVE INNOVATION IS THE KEY TO THE SUCCESS OF A BUSINESS ENTERPRISE

ZERO TO ONE
Author: Blake Masters and Peter Thiel
Genre: Business Management

No business book has had a more profound impact on me than "Zero to One" by Peter Thiel. This book is an absolute master-class in conducting business in the modern century. Peter is one of the most successful entrepreneurs in Silicon Valley who has laid the foundations for big enterprises like PayPal, Facebook, and Palantir Technologies. Through his intellect and disruptive thinking, he has made billions in the world of technology. He has passed on his learning, experience, wisdom and contrarian thinking through this book which has catapulted him to international stardom. This is one book that I can read over again and again. Let's discuss what makes this book such an amazing read.

He starts the book with some of the most pivotal lines I have ever read.

"Every moment in business happens only once. The next Bill Gates will not build an operating system. The next Larry Page or Sergey Brin won't make a search engine. And the next Mark Zuckerberg won't create a social network. If you are copying these guys, you aren't learning from them."

This is where he differentiates in what it means to go from "1 to n" and "0 to 1." He states that much of what happens in the world of business is copying or incremental changes, something which China is expert at. One good product is made and then innumerable products are made as its replicas. This is known as going from "1 to n" which does not lead to business sustainability and innovation since there is always someone behind you copying

your set of features in a much better way. He names this globalisation, which is not more than the mere spread of successful practices and technologies around the world. Organisations survive and thrive when they go from "0 to 1" and pursue disruptive innovation. When fresh, outrageous, unique and disruptive products are made having intrinsic proprietary advantage, they allow an organisation to grow exponentially.

Thiel states that globalisation vis-a-vis technology is not an important driver of progress. This is because globalisation simply uses existing technologies without working on newer ones. He advocates the fact that the key to all technological progress is a startup or new venture where a small group of people are aligned for a greater mission to make the world a better place.

He also explains in detail the ideology of competition and the beauty of monopoly which commonly tends to carry a negative connotation. In 2012, American airlines made on average 37 cents per passenger for each flight, despite the industry's revenue of $160 Billion. In the same year, Google had revenues of $50 Billion, of which 21 percent was pure profit. As a result, Google is worth more than all the airlines put together. The single biggest component which leads this differentiation is that Google has taken the game from "0 to 1" while the airline industry has fallen into the trap of "1 to n." What Google offers its customers through its most extensive suite of services, no one else can. Whereas, airlines more or less operate on relatively similar standards. This results in a situation of perfect competition which in turn leads to trivial profits. Whereas Google has created a monopoly not through any lobby or corruption but through its sheer disruptive thinking and innovative products. Thiel welcomes this sort of monopoly and thinks that this is what makes the world and companies move ahead. Great companies

Organisations survive and thrive when they go from "0 to 1" and pursue disruptive innovation. When fresh, outrageous, unique and disruptive products are made having intrinsic proprietary advantage, they allow an organisation to grow exponentially.

Great companies earn a monopoly by solving a unique problem while failed companies fail to escape the competition.

earn a monopoly by solving a unique problem while failed companies fail to escape the competition.

Now let's talk about what it takes to create a long-lasting and sustainable advantage and monopoly. This requires working on proprietary technology that is at least 10X (times) better than what anyone else is offering. This is what leading technology companies like Amazon, Facebook, Google and Microsoft do. The second feature of a proprietary product is economies of scale. These products or businesses get better and stronger as their size grows, they have absolutely no issues when it comes to scalability. He suggests new startup founders focus on creating new markets instead of running after an already saturated market full of competition. This is what Amazon's founder Jeff Bezos did by being the pioneer in selling books online and then slowly creating his own space around different things. Thiel also suggests to initially go for smaller markets since it is easier to dominate them rather than being a small fish in a big pond that is crowded with whales. He advises startup founders that instead of carrying an attitude of battling with incumbents and big guns in the business, focus on creating your own niche by offering something genuinely new.

Thiel is ruthless when it comes to pursuing innovation. He doesn't mince his words and stresses the fact that we are preached to make minimum viable products and iterate our way to success. He quotes the example of Apple and how it manages its schedule of products and innovation without depending on any focus groups. This is one of the biggest reasons which has contributed to its success. He discreetly states in the book that the best technology companies are not valued on the cash they are generating today, but on the number of subscribers, they will hold a decade from now.

A very important lesson that Peter Thiel gives in

this book is that a startup that is messed up at its foundation cannot be fixed. Therefore, it is of prime importance to select the right partner who will accompany you on the uncertain journey of starting your business.

Concluding his thoughts, he declares that the subject of Entrepreneurship can only be taught to a certain extent. There can be no guarantee of success. One can learn about the nuts and bolts of business through theoretical study but the creation and success of entrepreneurial ventures are still shrouded in mystery. However, he simultaneously offers a ray of hope that successful people find value in unexpected places, therefore, look for areas that the majority find stale and unattractive.

Successful people find value in unexpected places, therefore, look for areas that the majority find stale and unattractive.

Whenever someone asks me for a recommendation about books on entrepreneurship and startups my first recommendation is always "Zero to One." If you intend to have the best learning when it comes to startups or you aspire to be an entrepreneur in the future then Peter Thiel has given you an ultimate framework in the form of this masterpiece. Go and get it.

PERSONAL NOTES

Use this space to write your notes and key takeaways from the book.

REMEMBER, IT'S A SIN TO KILL A MOCKINGBIRD

TO KILL A MOCKINGBIRD
Author: Harper Lee
Genre: Fiction/Classics

There was a time when a major part of my reading haul was composed of fiction. I have read them all; Charles Dickens, Robert Louis Stevenson, Bronte sisters, Jane Austen, Mark Twain, Leo Tolstoy, and countless other stalwarts of literature. I feel it is indispensable that one should read fiction till at least the age of eighteen since it titillates the creative codes hidden inside our mind. I owe a lot of my cognitive development to the fantasy literature I read earlier on in my life. While there are many fiction books which I absolutely love, the one I want to discuss with you right now is 'To Kill A Mockingbird' by Harper Lee.

This book was an instant hit and made Harper Lee a household name. It is a classic of American literature which has influenced generations with its thought-provoking and profound underlying theme. To Kill A Mockingbird is loaded with lessons in humanity, equality, integrity and complex social webs which surround us. It gives a thumping lesson on how discrimination, prejudice and hatred are some of the worst afflictions that affect humanity. It very vividly highlights the pressing issues of rape and racism which corrodes our social ecosystem and makes the people of a certain stature vulnerable. Let me brief you on what the novel is all about.

The story spans the years of the Great Depression from 1933 to 1935. It revolves around a father named Atticus Finch and his two children Scout Finch and Jem Finch who live in a fictional town of Alabama. Atticus is a lawyer by profession. They have a mysterious neighbour named Boo Radley who is a recluse and there is a strange mystery

surrounding him. Both Scout and Jem develop an acquaintance with a boy named Dill and they start playing together.

One day, they discover that someone is leaving them gifts in a tree outside Radley's house. During this time, Boo Radley subliminally gives gestures of kindness and affection but overtly never comes in front of the children.

In parallel, Atticus Finch is given the task of defending a black man, Tom Robinson, who has been accused of raping a white woman. Majority of the citizens due to their inherent prejudice against the black people consider Tom the predator. However, Atticus Finch is a man of principles and he has a strong belief that Tom is innocent. This invites ridicule from society, as they start taunting the children that they and their father are "nigger lovers." The whole family is committed to the core to defend Tom and even suppress the mob that had come to lynch Tom to death.

During the trial, Atticus successfully establishes that Mayella had made sexual advances towards Tom. However, due to bias and prejudice against black people, Tom is convicted and sent to prison. Out of frustration and anxiety, her father is furious with Atticus for exposing him as a liar and an abuser. He vows revenge and plans to kill Scout and Jem. He attempts to stab them, but before he can do any further damage, Boo Radley intervenes and kills Bob Ewell. The Sheriff arrives and instead of taking Boo into custody, he weaves a story that Ewell fell on his own knife during the attack. Scout escorts Boo to his home after which he is never seen again.

This story packs a punch when read meticulously. Harper Lee has written her heart out. The way she narrates the story is mesmerising and keeps the reader engaged from the first to the last page. This

This story packs a punch when read meticulously. Harper Lee has written her heart out. The way she narrates the story is mesmerising and keeps the reader engaged from the first to the last page.

is one of the prime reasons why this book has been translated into over forty languages and has sold over 40 Million copies worldwide. The underlying racial injustice that permeates our society has been remarkably elaborated in the book.

The underlying racial injustice that permeates our society has been remarkably elaborated in the book.

The most famous quote from this book is "Remember, it's a sin to kill a mockingbird." It means that persecution of people who do not harm anyone in any way is a sin. It is the metaphor that has been used to depict the main storyline of the book.

What fascinated me the most is the way Harper Lee has demonstrated Atticus Finch's attitude towards his children. The way he has done their upbringing is something that every one of us should learn from in this novel. Another important lesson Atticus told his children was that before judging anyone, look at the world from their perspective i.e. develop empathy. Empathising with people in real life will actually solve a lot of our problems.

PERSONAL NOTES

Use this space to write your notes and key takeaways from the book.

PERSONAL NOTES

Use this space to write your notes and key takeaways from the book.

THE
GREATEST
ENTREPRENEURIAL
HUMAN
VENTURE

WORK RULES
Author: Laszlo Bock
Genre: Business Management

In the year 1998, two PhD students of Stanford University, Sergey Brin & Larry Page laid the foundations of a company which has today become an integral part of our lives. I don't think there is a day spent in our lives when we don't use the services of this company. No points for guessing friends, the name of this remarkable company is Google. Today, most probably there is no piece of information in this world which is not available on Google. With its starkly simple homepage, it has revolutionised the world and has become a gold standard for online search. Not only search, but there are numerous other products offered by Google that we use on daily basis like YouTube, Google Earth, Maps, Google Docs, Gmail, Android, Play Store, Photos, News, Travel, Translate, Google Fit and the list goes on. This is one company which has had the most profound impact on our lives.

Today, most probably there is no piece of information in this world which is not available on Google. With its starkly simple homepage, it has revolutionised the world and has become a gold standard for online search.

Being a global technology leader, it is the biggest desire of any software engineer or computer scientist to work at Google. One of the prime reasons for this is the amazing work environment that it offers which not only nurtures you professionally but also gives you an amazing lifestyle. The headquarter of Google known as Googleplex is a one-of-its-kind building. At Googleplex, employees' cycle around, get free meals, use slides instead of stairs, if they get bored play games like foosball or pool, exercise in the gym etc. This enjoyable and fun environment is not the only reason behind Google's success. There are some other very solid reasons which have contributed to its superstar status in the business world.

In the next few paragraphs, I will tell you seven unique things about this company which makes it a dream place to work at. You will also get to know about the attributes which you need to possess in order to be hired and be successful at Google.

Former Senior Vice President of Google, Laszlo Bock, has written a remarkable book titled "Work Rules" in which he has revealed the secrets which have made Google such a great company. It's such a well written book that I will advise every CEO and specially HR leaders to read it. Infact, I will go to this length to say that this 400-page book easily outweighs a 2-year MBA-HR program. It's a killer. Let's move towards the salient points described in the book.

It's such a well written book that I will advise every CEO and specially HR leaders to read it. Infact, I will go to this length to say that this 400-page book easily outweighs a 2-year MBA-HR program.

The biggest thing which stands out in Google is the opportunity that it gives its employees to be founders. Google doesn't treat its people like quintessential employees, rather every individual that works in the company feels like a founder who has tremendous authority to do work, run the team and set the culture of their department according to their will.

Google stands out because it provides an environment where every employee feels liberated to take independent decisions. Work culture is designed in a way where an individual working at Google, when he wakes up in the morning, feels as if he is not going for a job but for his own work. He takes ownership, has a sense of responsibility, feels empowered, has authority and is provided ample opportunities to grow. This is one of the reasons why Google is able to make such remarkable products.

Work culture is designed in a way where an individual working at Google, when he wakes up in the morning, feels as if he is not going for a job but for his own work.

Second best thing about this company is that it dovetails the work of every employee to the overall mission of the company. Google's mission is "to organise the world's information and make it universally accessible and useful." It seems to every

Google's mission is "to organise the world's information and make it universally accessible and useful."

employee working at Google that he is playing his role in making the world a better place. By doing this, they find meaning and purpose in their work which keeps them motivated 24/7/365. This is a very big reason behind the powerful culture at Google.

Third important thing about this company is its hiring mantra, which is: only hire people who are better than you. The recruitment process at Google is very lengthy and tedious and its reason is laser focus on onboarding quality human resources. There are no insecurities and fear in the HR experts and managers of this company when interviewing and selecting people. They make sure that the person who is hired has certain qualities which makes him better than them. Moreover, they hire A Graders (doesn't refer to academic grades) that's why they get A+ results.

Fourth unique and amusing practice which Google follows is that when a manager is being hired, his subordinates are also present in the interview. They are not only present passively, but their point of view matters a lot in the decision of whether that candidate will be hired or not. Run-of-the-mill companies cannot even think about this, but that's how Google works. This proves that Google is a non-hierarchical organisation where cronyism and nepotism have no place.

Fifth best thing about Google which is my most favorite is that its employees can spend 20% of their work week working on any project which is not related to their daily job. Googlers spend this time on projects which are of their own personal interest. To put the icing on the cake, Google not only gives them time to work on these projects but also invests in them. What a brilliant way of running the company, innovating and keeping the employees motivated simultaneously.

Google has a unique approach about the training of its employees as well. It believes that most of the companies waste billions of dollars on training without getting any significant results. In order to tackle this problem, Google has developed a culture whereby its own employees train their own people. Google thinks that it is the best approach, since no one knows its people and environment better than work colleagues. This approach gives the best returns on investment.

Seventh point is that Google believes in paying unfairly. This means that instead of grade and experience, employees salary will be commensurate to his contribution to the company. Most of the companies, specially in Pakistan, are usually stuck in grading structure. When it comes to rewarding employees, HR's vision is limited to saving the company's budget. This goes out of the window in the case of Google. They don't care about the budget; if a person is qualified, skilled and talented he is paid accordingly.

Now the question is in order to be hired at Google what personality attributes you need to possess? The first attribute is General Cognitive Ability, which means the capacity to reason, solve real life problems, plan, think abstractly, learn quickly and comprehend complex ideas. Google, instead of looking at your GPA and SAT score, judges you on your general intelligence. If your cognitive skills are strong, you can think loudly, can synthesise problems and solve them then you have a chance of being a Googler.

At Google, special emphasis is given to Leadership. It will be cliche to say that every organisation needs leaders. However, Google needs a specific type of leadership known as emergent leadership. This means leading without a title or a formal designation. Google believes that in the lifespan of a team, various leadership roles are required to be

Google, instead of looking at your GPA and SAT score, judges you on your general intelligence. If your cognitive skills are strong, you can think loudly, can synthesise problems and solve them then you have a chance of being a Googler.

Google needs a specific type of leadership known an emergent leadership. This means leading without a title or a formal designation.

filled in by different people. In these small ad hoc roles, they contribute, play their part and then recede back. Google wants its people to lead without a title.

The third attribute that Google looks for when hiring is, Googlyness. It means a likeable and fun-loving individual who is conscientious, has taken bold decisions in life and is comfortable in uncertainty. Google welcomes these sorts of people who have the ability to think at a different wavelength from general crowd.

The third attribute that Google looks for when hiring is, Googlyness. It means a likeable and fun-loving individual who is conscientious, has taken bold decisions in life and is comfortable in uncertainty.

The last attribute which is obvious is, role related knowledge. Since google is a technology company, it is in a constant search of technology experts who are champions in their field. They are on a constant hunt for people who are curious and can undertake things that no one has attempted before.

All of these attributes along with many others, have consolidated to make Google the best name in the industry in just a matter of a couple of decades. My final message to entrepreneurs is that most of the policies adopted by Google do not cost so much. You only need to possess the right attitude and vision to become a big company. You can also implement these practices in your organisation, whether it is big or small. Does your organisation follow any of the above practices? If yes, do they yield a desirable result?

PERSONAL NOTES

Use this space to write your notes and key takeaways from the book.

PERSONAL NOTES

Use this space to write your notes and key takeaways from the book.

MEN AND WOMEN THINK AND OPERATE DIFFERENTLY

MEN ARE FROM MARS, WOMEN ARE FROM VENUS

Author: John Gray
Genre: Psychology

Albert Einstein is one of the greatest stalwarts in the field of science. Almost all of us are aware about the great man due to his striking outlook and perennial presence in popular culture. He is known for his scientific theories such as the Special and General Theory of Relativity, Photoelectric Effect, Quantum Theory etc. However, there are a few peculiar things about his personal life that people in general are not aware of. One such remarkable thing was that Einstein had signed a contract with his wife which contained a strange clause which stated that, "You can't talk to me unless I want to talk to you." This means that his wife couldn't speak to him without his consent.

I have never heard something as bizarre as this in a marital relationship. The reason why I gave you the example of Einstein and his wife is because in the next few paragraphs, I will review a book which focuses on men and women especially in the context of a marital relationship. This book is so unique and meaningful that if its content is profoundly understood, men and women will never have any difficulty in understanding each other. There is hardly a book written on the personality and psychology of men and women that is more interesting, potent, effective and meaningful than "Men Are from Mars, Women Are from Venus" by John Gray.

This book describes the personality traits and psychology of men and women in such a beautiful, interesting and amusing way that one is left stunned and forced to think that how easy it is to understand his/her counterpart. Let's discuss some of the path

breaking discoveries mentioned in the book.

Women love to talk. There would have been countless times in your life where you would have heard women endlessly discussing a particular issue. Women are also experts in complaining perennially, specially matters of trivial importance (if you look at it from the perspective of man). As men, our natural reaction is immediately offering a solution to the problems women share with us. However, the amusing thing is that women do not need a solution; rather they just want someone to listen to them without offering a way out of the maze. That is how women are wired. Therefore, men need to develop patience capital and strong listening skills for their relationship to prosper. On the other hand, when men encounter a problem, they immediately try to find a solution without any consultation. While women iterate again and again and have several rounds of discussions with their partner or spouse before finding a solution. Thus, the advice for women is that whenever your husband has any problem don't give him unsolicited advice. Men don't like it. If your husband has any issues, try leaving him alone and give him some space. He will be ok.

As men, our natural reaction is immediately offering a solution to the problems women share with us. However, the amusing thing is that women do not need a solution; rather they just want someone to listen to them without offering a way out of the maze.

Whenever men undergo stress, they will become secluded, quiet and would want to be alone. Once a situation like this arises, wife tends to think that her husband doesn't love her anymore. He is not interested in me and doesn't want to live with me. These sort of assumption-based emotions trigger the problem whereas, the issue is very simple. Leave your husband alone and give him space when he is under stress or he will come out well. During this period do not stress, indulge in overthinking and stay relaxed.

Whenever men undergo stress, they will get secluded, quiet and would want to be alone. Once a situation like this arises, wife tends to think that her husband doesn't love her anymore. He is not interested in me and doesn't want to live with me.

Women's response to stress is quite the opposite. Instead of seclusion, they just want to talk and talk which men don't usually like. This in turn, leads to a conflict. Therefore, for men the advice is that

Women's response to stress is quite the opposite. Instead of seclusion, they just want to talk and talk which men don't usually like. This in turn, leads to a conflict.

whenever your partner is under stress try to maintain your patience level. Listen to her carefully and attentively, because that is what she wants.

The next point is perhaps the life and blood of this book which is "Men and women speak different languages." Men are always straightforward, objective and do not mince their words while women make optimum use of metaphors and exaggerations. You may have heard some women say these words: You always ignore me. You don't love me anymore. This house has become a garbage can. Your whole family is against me. We never go out to eat. The list is endless.

Superficially, these are quite negative utterings. However, if you dig deep, you will find that these statements carry subliminal messages. For example, when your wife says that "we never go out" this actually means that I'd love to be with you, so why not go out and spend some time together. If you fall for its superficial meaning, then a conflict is inevitable but if you understand its true meaning you will be able to tackle the situation really well. Similarly, when your wife says that the house is getting dirty and is in the worst condition, it means I'm very tired today and not feeling good. Don't expect that I'll clean the house today. Men in general tend to think that she is blaming us for the shabby condition of the house but as explained that's not actually what the case is.

Another aspect that John Gray discusses in this book is regarding the scoring system. Whenever men and women interact, they carry an invisible scoring system with them. This means that whenever one of them does a good job, they get a point. This seems very reasonable so far, but things get complex since the scoring criteria for men and women is totally different. For example, a husband plans a vacation in Thailand for his wife, takes her there, books the

best hotel, both go for a lot of shopping and have the time of their life. After so much of hard work and financial expense, man expects that he will get a lot of adulation and appreciation; but the poor guy gets just one point. Moreover, on returning home from his office, when the husband asks his wife how her day was and listens to her, he gets the same one point. Comparatively, there is no equivalence between a foreign trip vis-a-vis asking your wife how the day was, but that is how the scoring system works for women. The magnitude of the gift does not matter to women rather, the care and love of a man supersedes everything. A woman wants her husbands unshared, undivided attention and unconditional support. No matter how big a gift you give, small acts matter a lot.

So my dear book buddies this was a short summary of this very interesting book. It has amassed a huge following over the course of last many years due to its path breaking understanding of human nature and psychology. No wonder, John Gray has been able to sell millions of copies of this masterpiece. Do read it if you want to sustain your relationship and aspire to be the best friend of your spouse.

PERSONAL NOTES

Use this space to write your notes and key takeaways from the book.

MUSLIMS LOST THEIR TRACK WHEN THEY RELINQUISHED LEARNING AND EDUCATION

LOST ISLAMIC HISTORY
Author: Firas Al-Khateeb
Genre: History

Last year I had the opportunity to read a remarkable book recommended by Former Prime Minister Imran Khan titled "Lost Islamic History." This book was written by Firas Al-Khateeb in 2014. Firas Al-Khateeb is an American author who is an expert in Islamic history and what an amazing book he has written. It is a starkly honest and objective account of the reasons behind the rise and decline of Muslims. Lost Islamic History is a comprehensive crash course for those who do not know anything about Islamic history.

The book covers the last 1400 years in detail from the time of Prophet Muhammad (PBUH) all the way till modern times. It sheds light on the undaunted struggle of Prophet Muhammad (PBUH), how he spread the message of Islam, how did Islam spread after his demise, who were our Righteous Caliphs, how and why Islamic wars were fought, how the Umayyad dynasty, the Abbasid Caliphate, the Ottomans, the Mongols and the Mughals conducted their lives, how Muslim scientists led the world of science and what factors contributed towards the eventual decline of the Muslim Ummah. In the next few paragraphs, we will discuss three key takeaways from the book

1. How did Prophet Muhammad (PBUH) make Islam so popular in the Arab world?
2. From the 9th-13th century, what did Muslims scientists, philosophers and scholars do which stunned the world?
3. Why are Muslims in such a bad condition today?

I have extracted five main reasons from this book, which made the message of Islam spread so fast. The number one reason is that the Holy Prophet (PBUH) laid the foundation of the first egalitarian society based on equality, which had never happened in the past. A society in which there was social justice, equality, no discrimination, no hatred and no prejudice. A society where all people were equal.

The second reason for the quick spread of Islam was that Holy Prophet (PBUH) gave Arab society a new social order. Prior to Islam, Arabs were divided into different tribes and clans and always fought with each other. This changed dramatically after the arrival of Prophet Muhammad (PBUH). Especially, the farewell sermon of the Holy Prophet (PBUH) is a complete code of life which made people realise the importance of social harmony and unity.

The third major reason for the spread of Islam was the attitude of Muslims towards non-Muslims. In the welfare state of Medina, Jews and people from other religions had complete liberty and freedom to practice their religion. Due to the tolerant attitude of Muslims, they had no pressure on them to accept Islam. This promoted pluralism in the society which eventually developed people's interest in the peaceful message of Islam.

The fourth major reason was that for the first time in human history rights of women were overtly made part of social fabric of the society. This included their participation in the society as well as their share in property. The fifth and from my point of view the biggest reason behind the spread of Islam were the teachings of Holy Prophet (PBUH) which taught the people how to deal with each other. He taught the people how to conduct their life, how to build a community, how to shape people's attitudes, how to negotiate, how to trade and how to live in harmony and peace. The best thing about this whole exercise

was that he led all this from the front through his own acts. He presented himself as a benchmark through which people can learn and improve their lives.

Now let's talk about the scientific and scholarly feats that Muslims achieved between 9th-13th century which elevated them as leaders of the world. The foundation for this work was laid by Caliph Al-Mamun, the seventh Abbasid Caliphate. Caliph Al-Mamun's thought process was very unique and progressive. He believed that if an ideal, modern society was to be created, Muslims would have to focus on research, especially science. He followed the hadith of the Holy Prophet (PBUH) in which he said that "Allah makes the way to Paradise easy for those who follow the path of knowledge." In addition, Islam as a religion states that research, knowledge and learning is an act of worship.

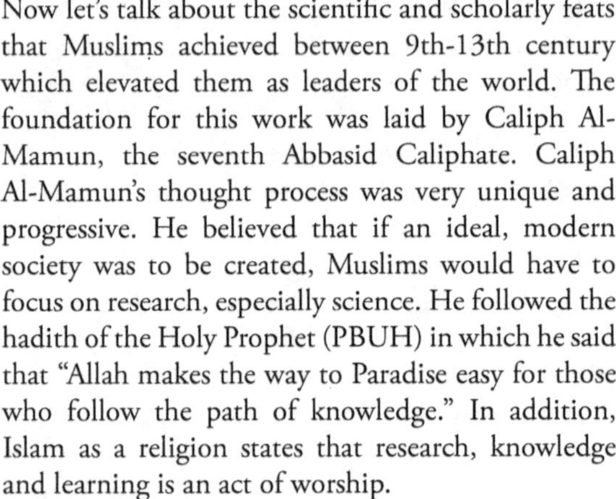

Caliph Al-Mamun's thought process was very unique and progressive. He believed that if an ideal, modern society was to be created, Muslims would have to focus on research, especially science.

Caliph Al-Mamun soon realised that the scientific knowledge was scattered throughout the Islamic Empire. He contemplated establishing a Centre, where Muslim scholars from all over the world would gather and share their knowledge and wisdom. With this in mind, he created a university, a library and an institute named "Bait-ul-Hikmah" which means "House of Wisdom." Bait-ul-Hikmah attracted scholars from all over the world where they would discuss ideas, disseminate knowledge and work on new inventions.

Due to the vision of Caliph Al-Mamun, Muslim scientists went on to become the most sought-after intellectuals of those times. Muhammad Ibn Musa al-Khwarizmi developed Algebra and introduced zero in mathematics. Omar Khayyam, who is known as a poet in the West, devised methods to solve cubic equations. Al-Battani developed Trigonometry. Al-Beruni wrote two books and for the first time stated that the earth rotates around its axis. The most

breathtaking thing about Al-Beruni is that without the use of modern scientific equipment he calculated the circumference of Earth at Pind Dadan Khan (Pakistan) with 99% accuracy.

Muslim geographers also found out the diameter of the earth. Muhammad Ali Idrisi created the world's first modern atlas and created a world map. Al-Razi discovered cures for coughs, headaches and constipation. Ibn e Sīnā authored a book, The Canon of Medicine, which is considered a medical encyclopedia. In addition, he discovered for the first time, that if you have negative thoughts in your mind they can lead to physical illnesses. This means that hundreds of years back Muslim scientists laid the foundation of psychology as well.

There was also a great Muslim scientist named Ibn Al-Haytham, who worked on the nature of light. He is also considered as the founder of Optics. He wrote about 200 books and invented the pinhole camera as well. This suggests that when Europe was reeling through the Dark Ages, Muslims were at the peak of their intellectual capacity and contributed in all fields of science as pioneers.

Now let's talk about the reasons behind the decline of Muslims. Firas Al-Khateeb in the eleventh chapter of the book states that the central theme of our religion is that it is complete and perfect. We have the Holy Quran and Hadiths. Despite all of this, why are Muslims in such a bad condition across the globe? Why is the Muslim Ummah suffering from so many challenges? Why we are not united? Why are we so far behind the West?

He states two pivotal reasons behind this decline. First is the loss of military power over the course of history. Muslims were the ones who invented war artillery technology specially pertaining to canons. However, Europeans adopted it, made it better and

The most breathtaking thing about Al-Beruni is that without the use of modern scientific equipment he calculated the circumference of Earth at Pind Dadan Khan (Pakistan) with 99% accuracy.

331

eventually used it against the Muslim world. The second main reason which I fully agree with is that there has been an intellectual decline amongst the Muslims since 13th century onwards. Tell me one thing of value that Muslims have invented in the last 800 years? Europe invented the printing press, disseminated knowledge, escaped the conservative church and developed themselves into the leaders of the world. On the other hand, Muslims were left far behind after declaring the printing press as un-Islamic.

The modern century demands moving ahead with time and being progressive. Only those nations and countries will prosper and stay relevant who adopt modern knowledge and possess a learning attitude. It is high time that the Muslim world realises this fact and starts acting on it. Otherwise, 1000 more years will pass by and the Muslim world will continue to struggle from stagnancy and bankruptcy of ideas.

PERSONAL NOTES

Use this space to write your notes and key takeaways from the book.

AFTERWORD - AUTHOR'S NOTE

I found great joy in writing "Readistan." The words which constitute this book have originated from the core of my heart. I hope the pages that you read in my book have helped you learn new things and will leave an impact on your heart and mind. As I have mentioned time and again in the book, I am a strong believer in the fact that lifelong learning and evolution of ideas keep an individual relevant across all generations. The reason for this is that the speed at which the world is changing has made it indispensable for us to be on our toes and broaden our horizon of thinking and learning.

This book is a step in this direction. The objective of imparting knowledge and wisdom has become one of the ultimate aims of my life and I intend to continue it till I breathe my last. I feel that life is worthless if it is not utilised to provide benefit to the people around you. It is my honest intention to build a large community of people who believe in positive discourse, pursue progressive ideas and are in the perennial pursuit of acquiring knowledge. I have sincere hope from you as a reader that you will continue to support my honest endeavour and advocate my thought process to the people around you so that together we can continue to grow. Share this book as a gift with your near and dear ones. They won't regret it.

My best wishes are with all of you.

Shah Rukh Nadeem